HOW IT WORKS

INSECTS

GERALD LEGG

award

Series Editor: Elizabeth Miles
Illustrations: Steve Weston
Additional illustrations: Ruth Lindsay, Jim Channell
Photography and additional illustrations: Shutterstock.com (Mikado767, Aksenova Natalya, Yusnizam Yusof, irin-k, Juraj Kovac, D. Kucharski K. Kucharska, Vladimirkarp, suns07butterfly, Malachi Jacobs, Sergey Toronto, Ultraviolet_Photographer, Cherdchai Chaivimol, alslutsky, bluehand, pzAxe, Africa Studio, Protasov AN, Kirsanov Valeriy Vladimirovich, Super Prin, IrinaK, Tyler Fox, Matt Jeppson, Shutter Rich, Cosmin Manci, goldenjack, epioxi, Pavel Krasensky, Eric Isselee, SSalparadis, Hector Ruiz Villar, thomas eder, DJTaylor, MeggedyannePhotography, PHOTO FUN, Pavel Mikoska, Scadidi, khunkorn, thatmacroguy, HHelene, yusuf kurnia), Ajcoyote (CC BY-SA 3.0), Greg Hume (CC-BY-2.5)

ISBN 978-1-78270-000-5

Copyright © Award Publications Limited

All rights reserved. No part of this publication may be reproduced or utilised in any form or by any means electronic or mechanical, including photocopying, recording, or by any information storage and retrieval system now known or hereafter invented, without the prior written permission of the publisher.

This edition first published 2025

Published by Award Publications Limited,
The Old Riding School, Welbeck,
Worksop, S80 3LR

/awardpublications   @award.books
www.awardpublications.co.uk

23-1100 1

Printed in China

Contents

What is an Insect?	6	New Life	28
Armour Plating	8	Changing Shape	30
Insect Eyes	10	Ant Nest	32
Feelers	12	Bee Nest	34
Flying	14	Rainforest Life	36
Hunting	16	Insects in Water	38
Self-defence	18	Woodland Life	40
Colour and Shape	20	Desert Insects	42
Feeding	22	Microscopic Life	44
Parasites	24	Index	46
Mating	26		

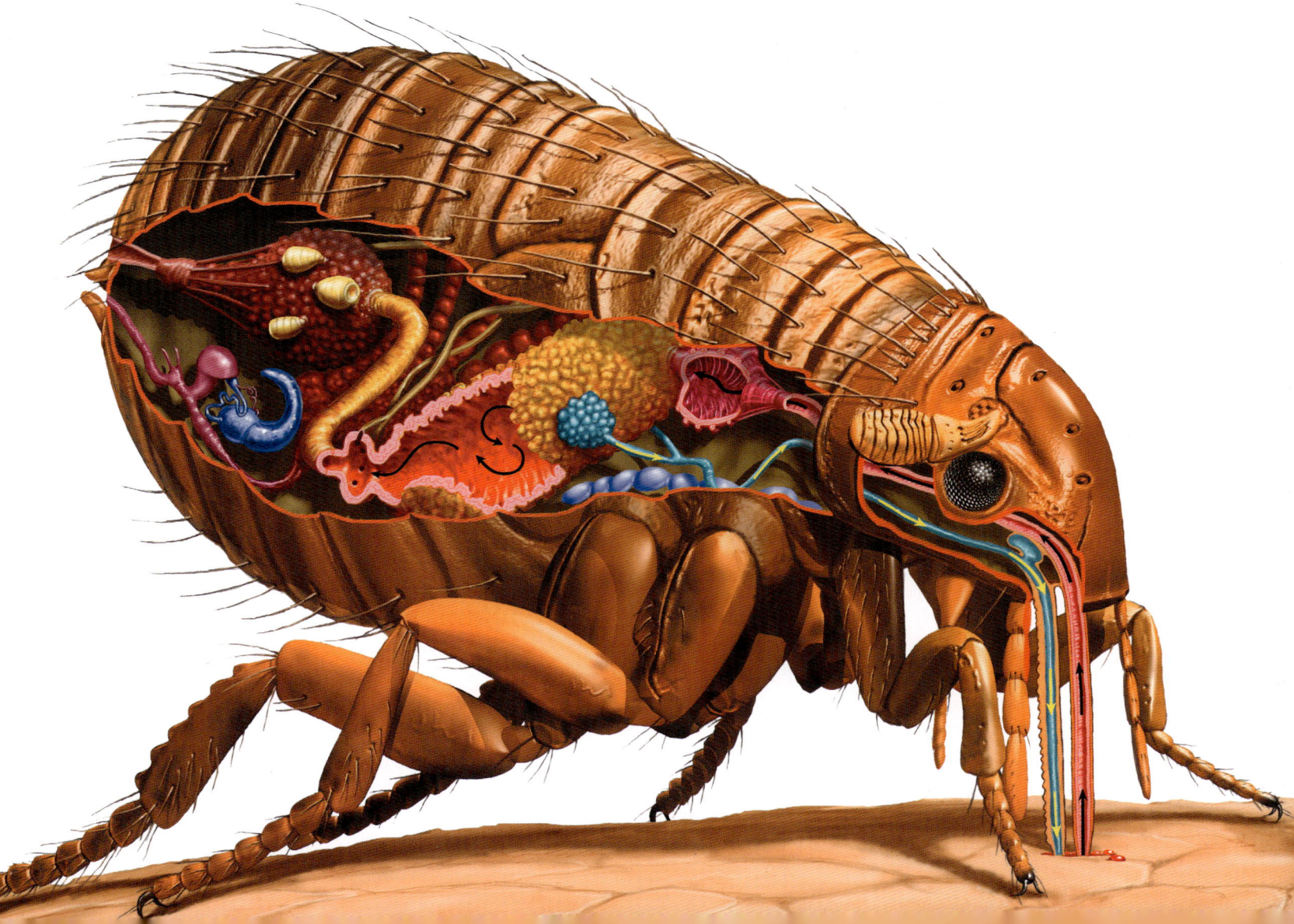

What is an Insect?

There are more insects on Earth than any other type of creature. Insects are strong and small, with three pairs of legs but no backbone. Like knights in armour, they have a tough outer covering. This outer skeleton (exoskeleton) supports and protects the insect's body parts and soft insides.

The protected head of an insect holds the brain and carries the antennae, eyes, mouth and special jaws. Different insects have differently shaped jaws, allowing them to eat all kinds of things. The abdomen contains the main organs, including those for digesting food. Throughout the body, special breathing tubes called trachea carry air to and from the body's tissues. A long, thin heart circulates blood. A nerve cord that controls various body processes runs from the brain to the tip of the abdomen.

How does a locust jump?

The locust sits, folding the two large joints of its back legs together. Inside each leg, strong muscles rapidly contract (shorten), causing the legs to straighten. This catapults the locust into the air, ready to fly or land some distance away.

Food passes into the gizzard where it is ground up and filtered

The crop receives and stores the food to be digested

Blood is pumped around the body by the heart

The locust's thin, flexible antennae are sensitive to smells

Each compound eye is made up of hundreds of light-sensitive units

Every part of the body is covered by the exoskeleton consisting of cuticle, which is made up of layers of protein and a hard layer of chitin

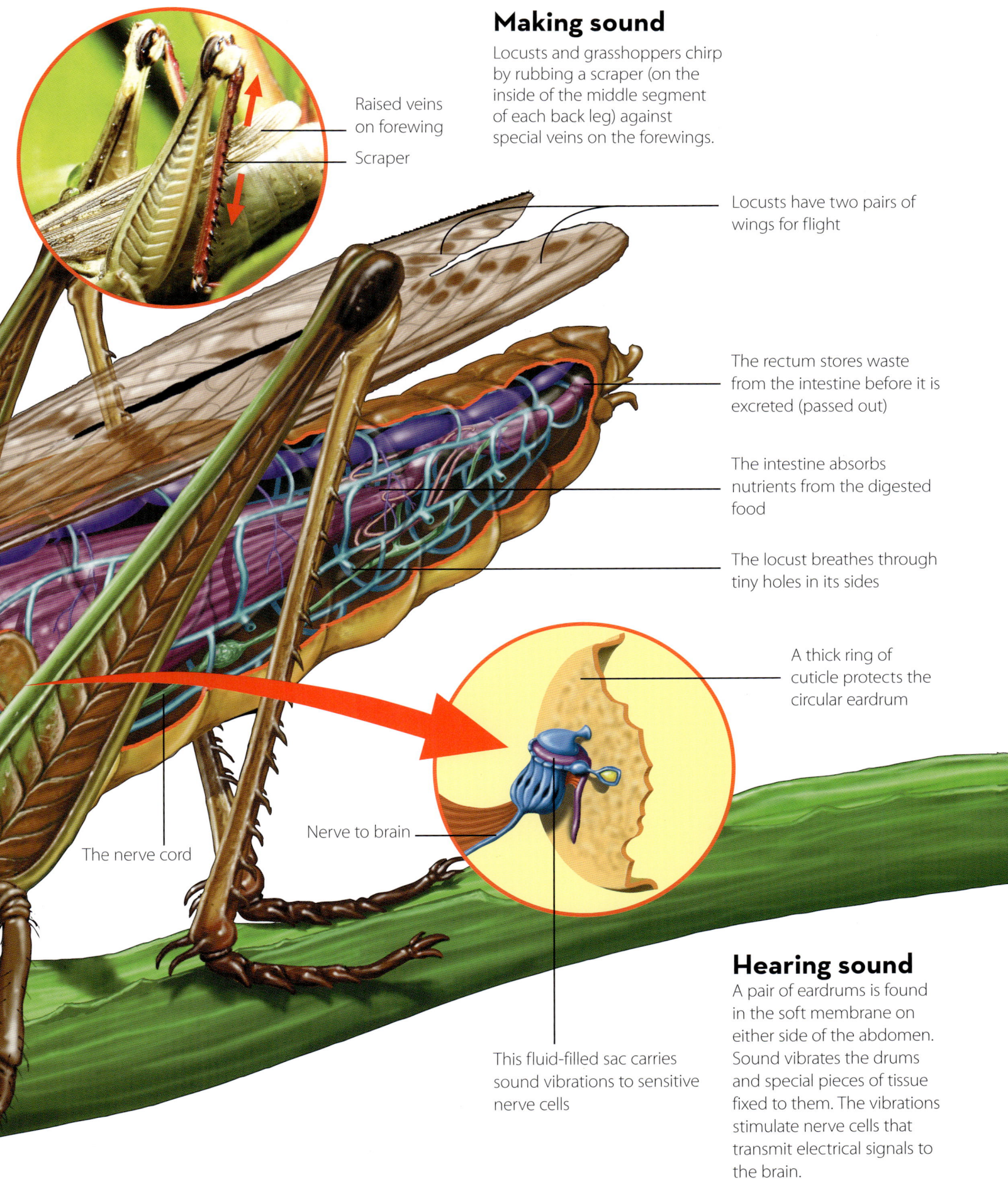

Armour Plating

Insects wear their skeleton on the outside, like armour. This exoskeleton is what makes insects so good at survival, even in conditions that are too extreme for other kinds of animal. Made of cuticle, it is tough and skin-like, protecting the organs and supporting the muscles. The cuticle itself consists of layers of protein and a layer of ultra-hard chitin.

Insects' jaws are covered in cuticle that is very hard, except at the joints, where it is soft and flexible. Thin tubes of cuticle make strong, jointed legs. The head and thorax are like boxes made of thick cuticle.

The head protects the brain and carries the sense organs and mouth parts. The strong thorax supports the wing and leg muscles. In contrast, the abdomen, which holds most of the body organs, is flexible and made of rings of cuticle, called segments.

Beetle

There are over 350,000 species of beetle ranging in size from 0.5 mm to over 170 mm. They are found everywhere. Hard, tough forewings protect their delicate flying wings. Shown here is a spotted flower beetle.

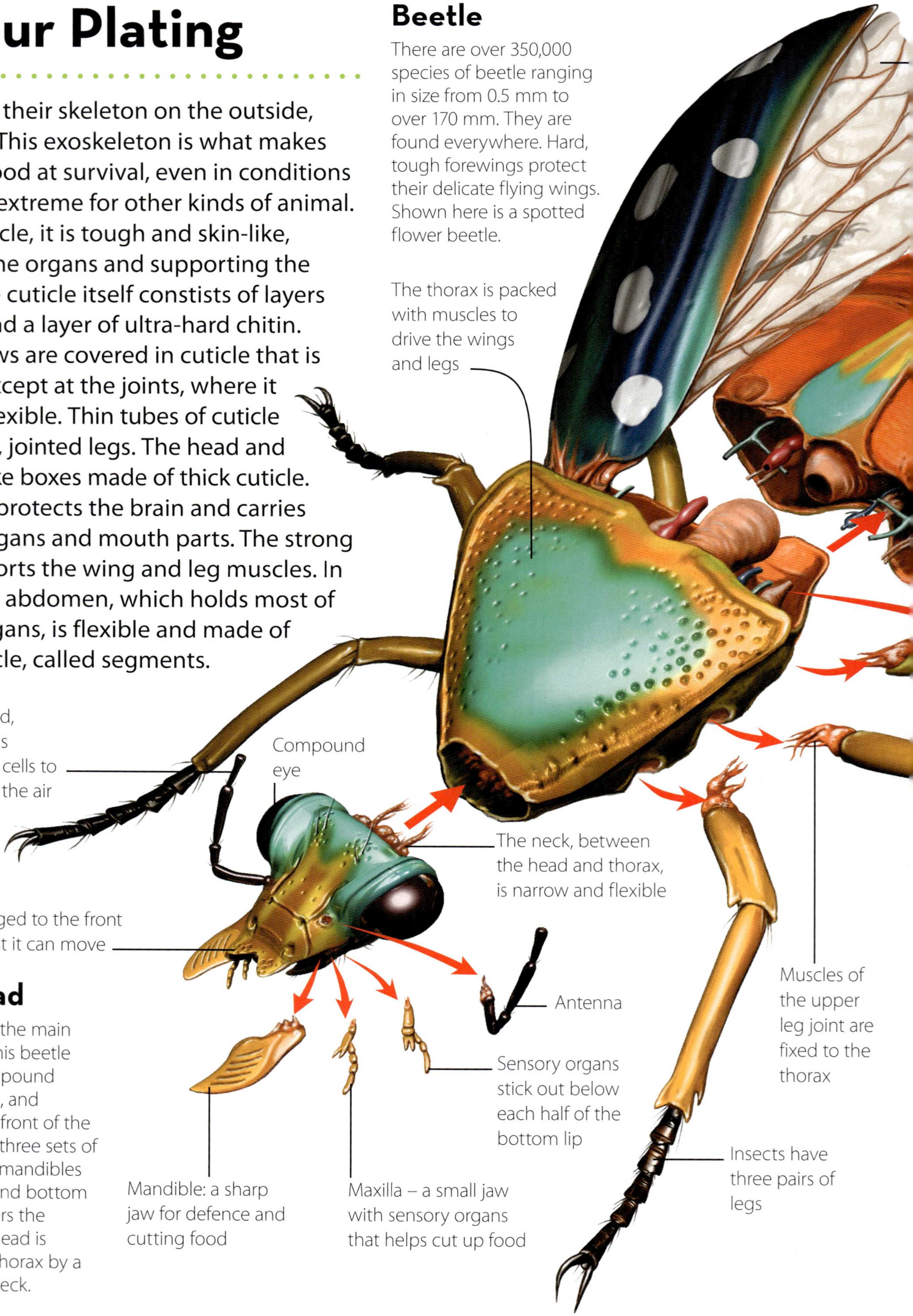

The thorax is packed with muscles to drive the wings and legs

Each multi-jointed, flexible antenna is covered in sense cells to detect odours in the air

Compound eye

The neck, between the head and thorax, is narrow and flexible

The top lip is hinged to the front of the face so that it can move

Antenna

Muscles of the upper leg joint are fixed to the thorax

Insect head

The head carries the main sense organs – this beetle has a pair of compound eyes, simple eyes, and antennae. At the front of the mouth there are three sets of mouthparts: the mandibles (jaws), maxillae and bottom lip. A top lip covers the mandibles. The head is attached to the thorax by a narrow, flexible neck.

Mandible: a sharp jaw for defence and cutting food

Maxilla – a small jaw with sensory organs that helps cut up food

Sensory organs stick out below each half of the bottom lip

Insects have three pairs of legs

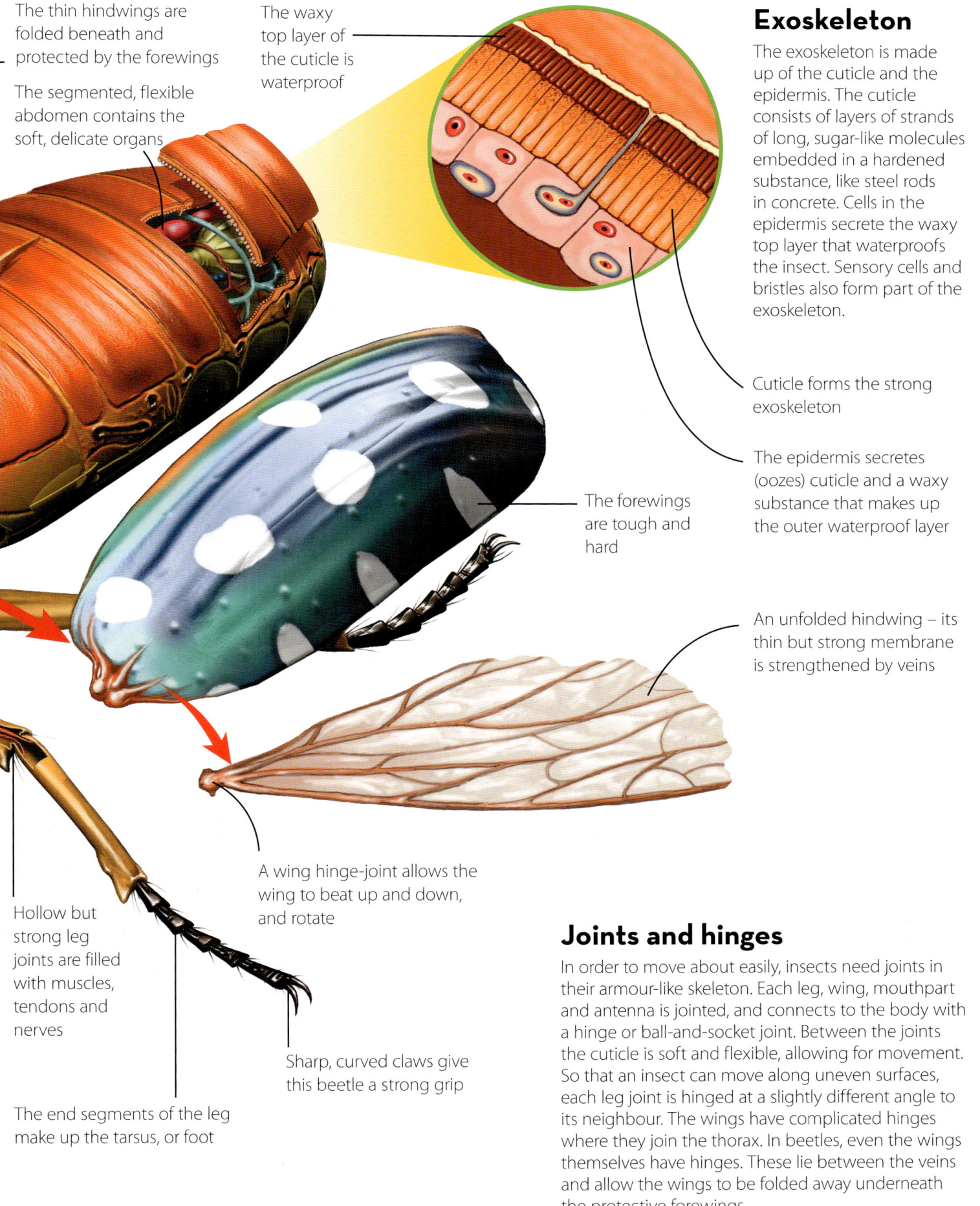

The thin hindwings are folded beneath and protected by the forewings

The segmented, flexible abdomen contains the soft, delicate organs

The waxy top layer of the cuticle is waterproof

Exoskeleton

The exoskeleton is made up of the cuticle and the epidermis. The cuticle consists of layers of strands of long, sugar-like molecules embedded in a hardened substance, like steel rods in concrete. Cells in the epidermis secrete the waxy top layer that waterproofs the insect. Sensory cells and bristles also form part of the exoskeleton.

Cuticle forms the strong exoskeleton

The epidermis secretes (oozes) cuticle and a waxy substance that makes up the outer waterproof layer

The forewings are tough and hard

An unfolded hindwing – its thin but strong membrane is strengthened by veins

A wing hinge-joint allows the wing to beat up and down, and rotate

Hollow but strong leg joints are filled with muscles, tendons and nerves

Sharp, curved claws give this beetle a strong grip

The end segments of the leg make up the tarsus, or foot

Joints and hinges

In order to move about easily, insects need joints in their armour-like skeleton. Each leg, wing, mouthpart and antenna is jointed, and connects to the body with a hinge or ball-and-socket joint. Between the joints the cuticle is soft and flexible, allowing for movement. So that an insect can move along uneven surfaces, each leg joint is hinged at a slightly different angle to its neighbour. The wings have complicated hinges where they join the thorax. In beetles, even the wings themselves have hinges. These lie between the veins and allow the wings to be folded away underneath the protective forewings.

Insect Eyes

Insects have two types of eyes. The largest are the compound eyes that appear as a honeycomb pattern of hexagons when seen under a microscope. Each hexagon is the transparent cuticle of an individual organ of sight. Insects can have as many as 30,000 of these in each compound eye or as few as one. Each of these sight organs (called ommatidia) sees only a tiny part of the surroundings. But as the tiny images are merged in the brain, the insect is able to see all around in great detail.

The second type of eyes, called ocelli, are usually much smaller. They are similar to human eyes, but cannot see an image. Instead, they are very sensitive to light. Nocturnal insects, which are active at night, have very large ocelli.

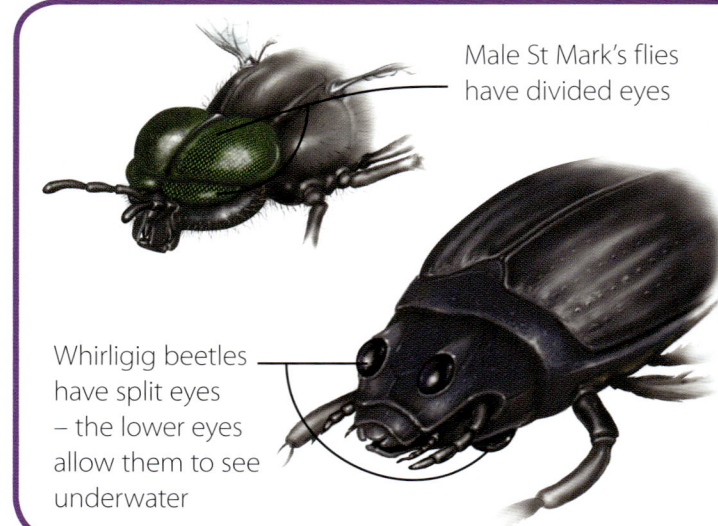

Male St Mark's flies have divided eyes

Whirligig beetles have split eyes – the lower eyes allow them to see underwater

Ommatidia

Light from the outside world enters each ommatidium and is focused by a hexagonal lens. It then passes through the crystal-like cone that also helps to focus it. Next, it reaches the nerve cells, which have a light-sensitive inner part. From here, the light is carried by nerve fibres to the brain. Pigment cells surround the nerve cells and stop light leaking into the rest of the eye, as this would spoil the image.

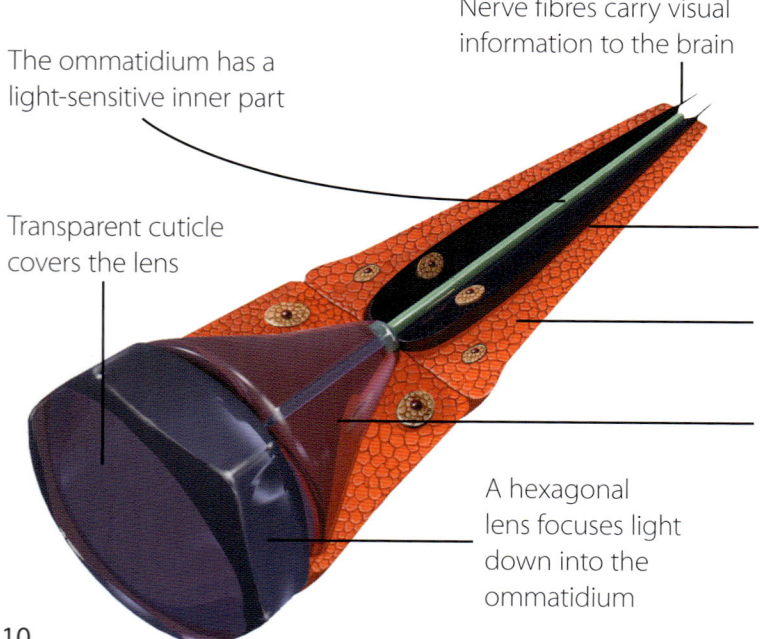

The ommatidium has a light-sensitive inner part

Transparent cuticle covers the lens

Nerve fibres carry visual information to the brain

Nerve cell

Pigment cells keep light inside the ommatidium

The crystal-like cone is surrounded by pigment cells

A hexagonal lens focuses light down into the ommatidium

Unusual eyes

Whirligig beetles live on the surface of ponds. Their eyes are split, with one pair on top and the other underneath. This lets them see above and below the water's surface at the same time. The eyes of male St Mark's flies are divided into an upper part with large ommatidia and a lower part with small ommatidia.

Damselfly

Damselflies are delicate but agile hunters. Large compound eyes (1) provide very clear, all-round vision. Light-sensitive ommatidia (2) send their mass of signals down the huge optic nerves (3) to the brain (4), which analyses information from all the senses. The damselfly's three small ocelli (5) are sensitive to light intensity. They are situated between the widely spaced compound eyes.

The two short antennae can sense smells

The shimmering, colourful compound eyes are made up of thousands of hexagonal lenses

Widely spaced eyes make it easier to judge distances

The ends of the ommatidia are connected to the optic nerves inside the fly's head

Mouthparts for eating prey

Invisible colour

Many insects can see ultraviolet, a colour invisible to us. Some flowers reflect this colour so that insects can see special markings that will guide them to the flower's nectaries.

11

Feelers

Insect feelers are remarkable instruments. The two feelers (antennae) are covered in many thousands of sensory cells, which can detect tiny amounts of chemicals, even a single molecule. This means, for example, that a male moth can detect the scent of a female moth that is over a kilometre away.

Insects can even 'see' using their feelers, mapping out the shape of their surroundings from the smells in it. Insects use sensory cells to find their way about and to find many other things: a mate; the right plant on which to lay their eggs; tasty prey, or a good host to live on. Although insects have other chemical-sensitive organs, such as taste organs, these are not as sensitive and need direct contact with a substance.

Each joint of the antenna shaft has four fine branches

Feathery branches provide room for numerous sense organs

The legs and body are covered in a thick mass of 'hairs', which makes for silent flight

Large eyes for seeing in low light levels

Emperor moths include the largest moths – some have a wingspan of up to 30 centimetres

Types of feelers

① ② ③ ④ ⑤ ⑥ ⑦

Feelers come in a great variety of shapes and sizes, especially in the beetle world. Springtails and dragonflies have thread-like feelers (**1**). Some ground beetles have a saw-edge variety (**2**). Termites and earwigs have bead-like ones (**3**) and those of burying beetles are clubbed (**4**).

Sawflies and cardinal beetles have feather-like feelers (**5**) and the cockchafer beetle and june bug have feather-tipped ones (**6**). Weevils and parasitic wasps have flexible 'elbowed' feelers (**7**).

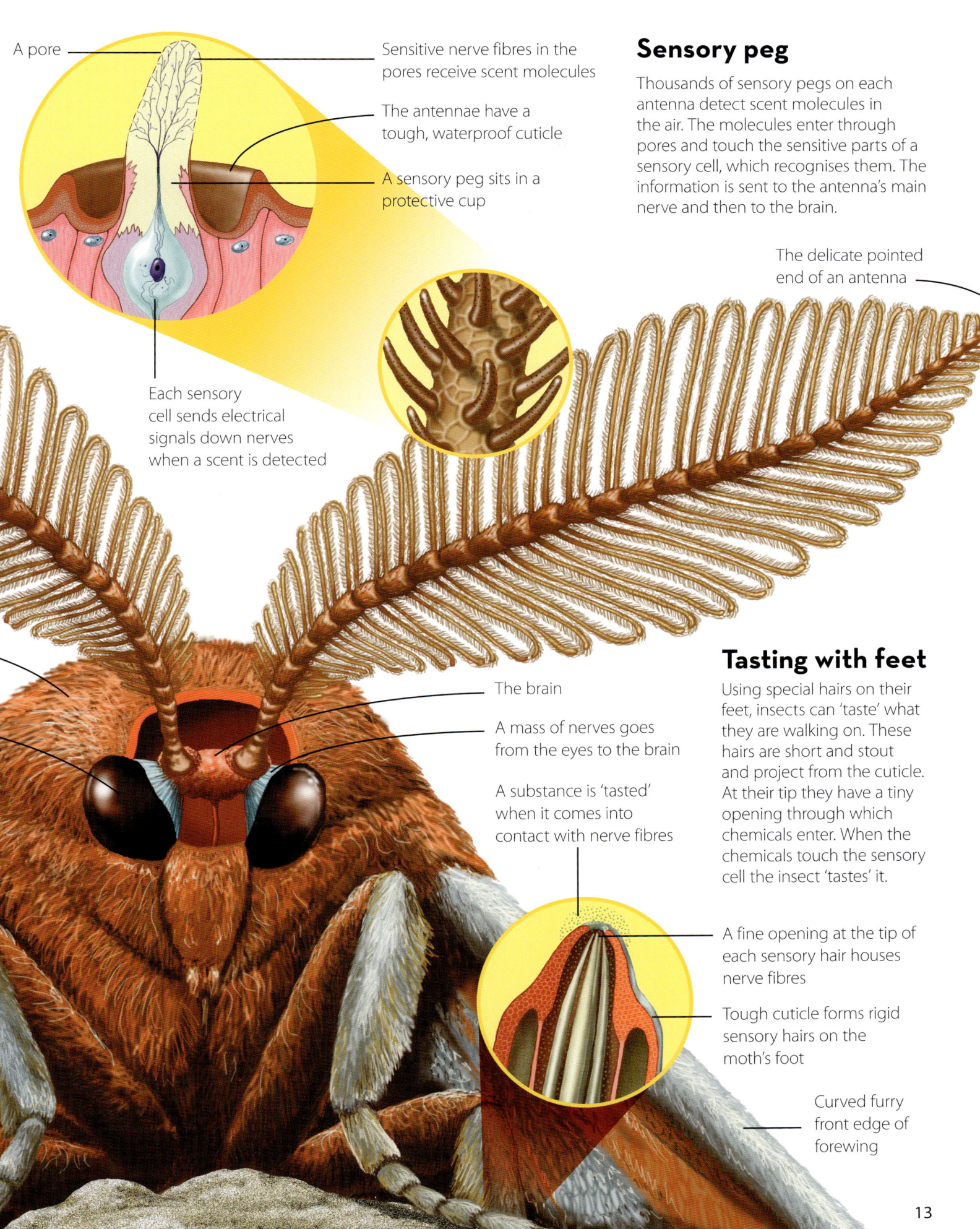

Flying

Insects can perform almost any flying manoeuvre – forwards, backwards, sideways, or upside down. They can loop, hover, swoop, and even do vertical take-offs. An insect's thorax is an extremely complicated, tough – but flexible – powerhouse, packed with muscles that control the movement of the wings. Each wing is hinged to the thorax by ball-and-socket joints that pivot near the inner end of the wing.

When the wing moves, it rocks on these joints like a seesaw that can swivel in all directions. To move their wings, some insects, including dragonflies, use muscles fixed directly to the end of their wings. Most other insects use muscles that are fixed to the top and bottom and the front and back of the thorax.

As the wasp moves forwards and lifts into the air, its wings beat up and down

Linked pairs
Wings that are linked together make for efficient flight. Butterflies link their wings by overlapping them, and wasps have hooks on their hindwing that hook into a fold on the forewing.

Each pair of wings is linked together, giving extra lift

The wing tilts with the leading edge facing downwards

Veins give the wing strength and shape for efficient flight

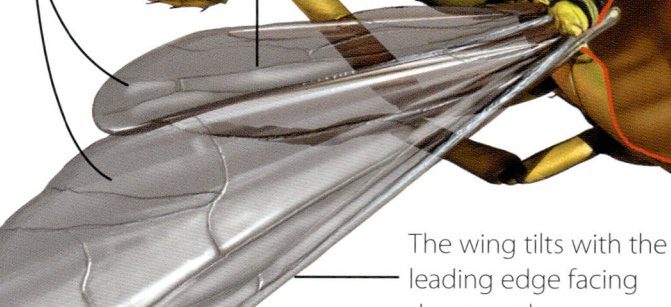

Wing types
The dragonfly (**1**) has two pairs of wings that move alternately. They are driven by muscles fixed directly to the wings. A butterfly (**2**) has slow-beating wings that overlap – the front wing pulls the back one down. Flies (**3**) use one pair of wings for flying, and a second pair form special organs for controlling flight. Beetles (**4**) have tough front wings that protect the delicate hindwings when they are folded away.

Wing down
Many insects, like this wasp, move their wings down by contracting (shortening) the thorax muscles that run front-to-back and relaxing (lengthening) those that run top-to-bottom. This makes the thorax bulge. The thorax cuticle (outer covering) is like tough elastic, so when it bulges, the wings are flicked down.

On the upstroke, the wing tilts upwards

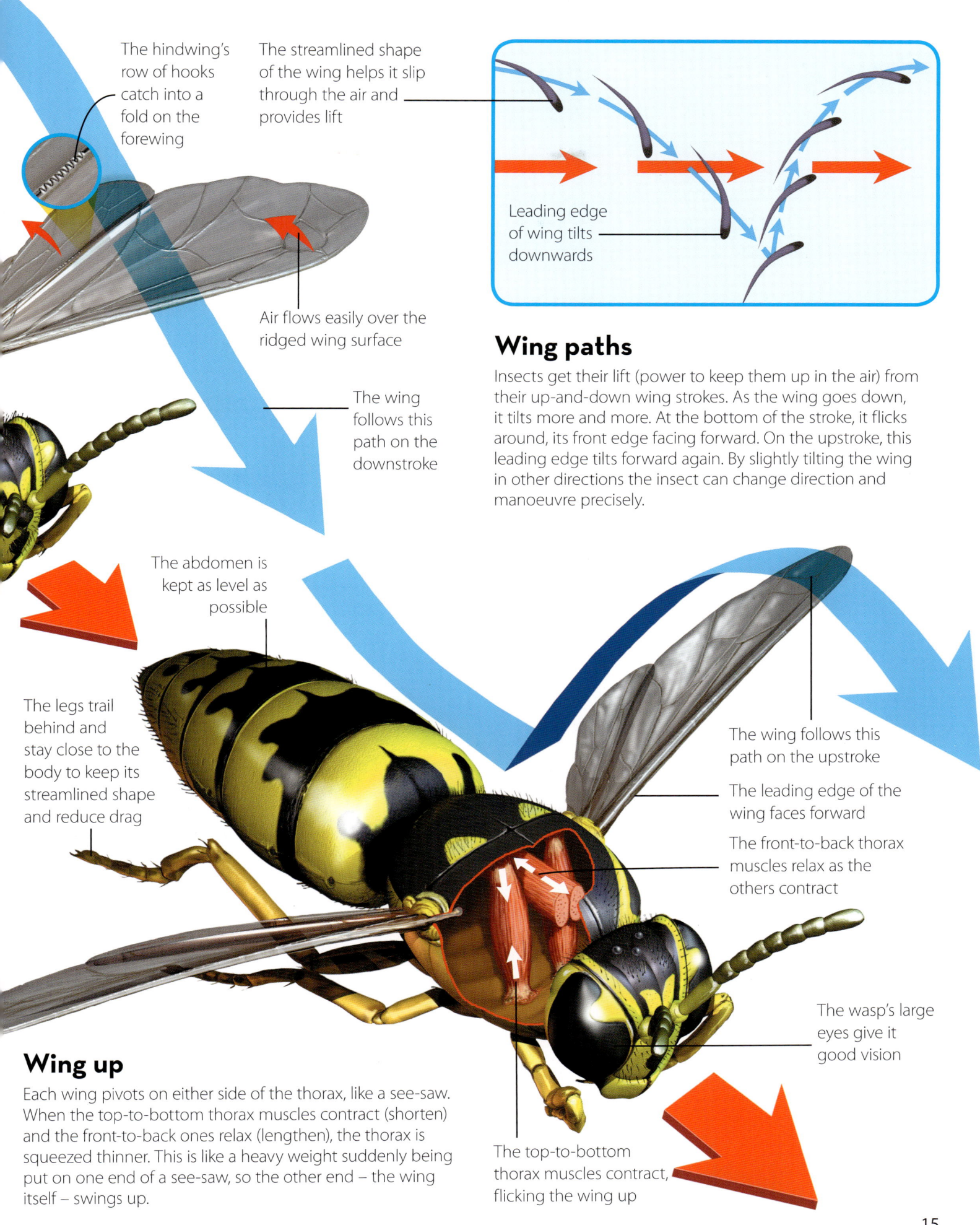

The hindwing's row of hooks catch into a fold on the forewing

The streamlined shape of the wing helps it slip through the air and provides lift

Air flows easily over the ridged wing surface

The wing follows this path on the downstroke

Leading edge of wing tilts downwards

Wing paths

Insects get their lift (power to keep them up in the air) from their up-and-down wing strokes. As the wing goes down, it tilts more and more. At the bottom of the stroke, it flicks around, its front edge facing forward. On the upstroke, this leading edge tilts forward again. By slightly tilting the wing in other directions the insect can change direction and manoeuvre precisely.

The abdomen is kept as level as possible

The legs trail behind and stay close to the body to keep its streamlined shape and reduce drag

The wing follows this path on the upstroke

The leading edge of the wing faces forward

The front-to-back thorax muscles relax as the others contract

The wasp's large eyes give it good vision

The top-to-bottom thorax muscles contract, flicking the wing up

Wing up

Each wing pivots on either side of the thorax, like a see-saw. When the top-to-bottom thorax muscles contract (shorten) and the front-to-back ones relax (lengthen), the thorax is squeezed thinner. This is like a heavy weight suddenly being put on one end of a see-saw, so the other end – the wing itself – swings up.

Hunting

Predators need quick reactions and speed to catch wary or fast-moving prey. They are armed with powerful jaws, designed to capture, kill, and cut up their meal. Praying mantises (*right*) use their special front legs to catch their victims before biting their prey into pieces with their jaws.

Many insects are active hunters, prowling around looking for suitable prey. Others, such as mantises, employ a wait-and-see method. They patiently keep still until their victim comes within range, and then pounce on it. Such ambush hunters are well-camouflaged to avoid being spotted by their victims until it is too late.

Wait and see

A praying mantis keeps perfectly still, close to somewhere that its prey is likely to land. Its legs are bent, ready to pounce.

The eyes of the mantis are fixed on its prey

Balanced on its hind legs, the mantis is ready to pounce

The leaf perch helps as camouflage

In for the kill

The patience of the praying mantis is rewarded. With its keen vision, the praying mantis spots a bee landing on a flower. Using its claws, the mantis firmly grips its perch. Then, in the blink of an eye, its powerful back legs catapult its body forwards. At the same time, it shoots out its front legs and grabs the helpless victim, which has no time to avoid the unexpected, deadly lunge.

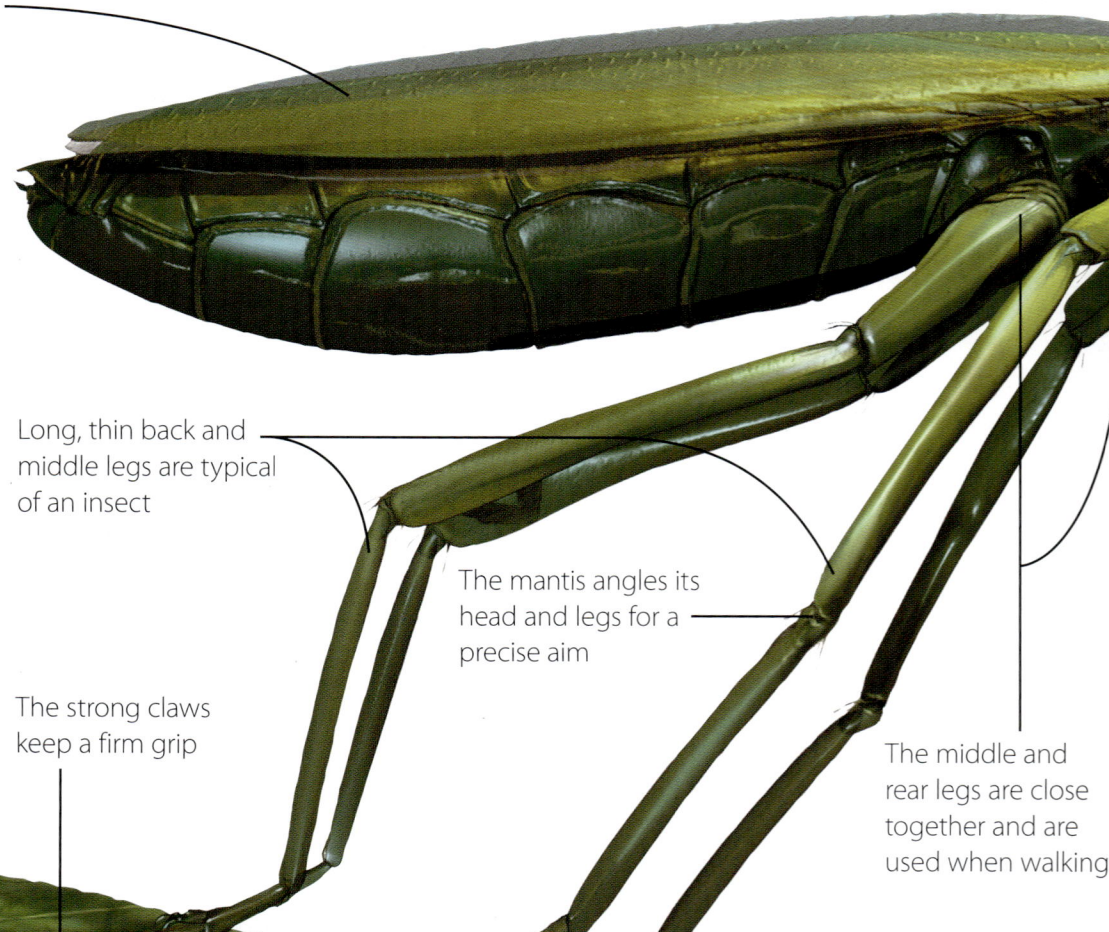

The long, thin body and wings of the mantis resemble a plant

Long, thin back and middle legs are typical of an insect

The mantis angles its head and legs for a precise aim

The strong claws keep a firm grip

The middle and rear legs are close together and are used when walking

The prey, unaware of danger, has just landed on a flower

Powerful jaws

Soldier ant   Tiger beetle   Stag beetle

Insect jaws have many uses. Soldier ants use them to catch food and to defend their colony. Tiger beetles use their jaws to catch their prey. The stag beetle's huge jaws are used in fighting and to attract a mate.

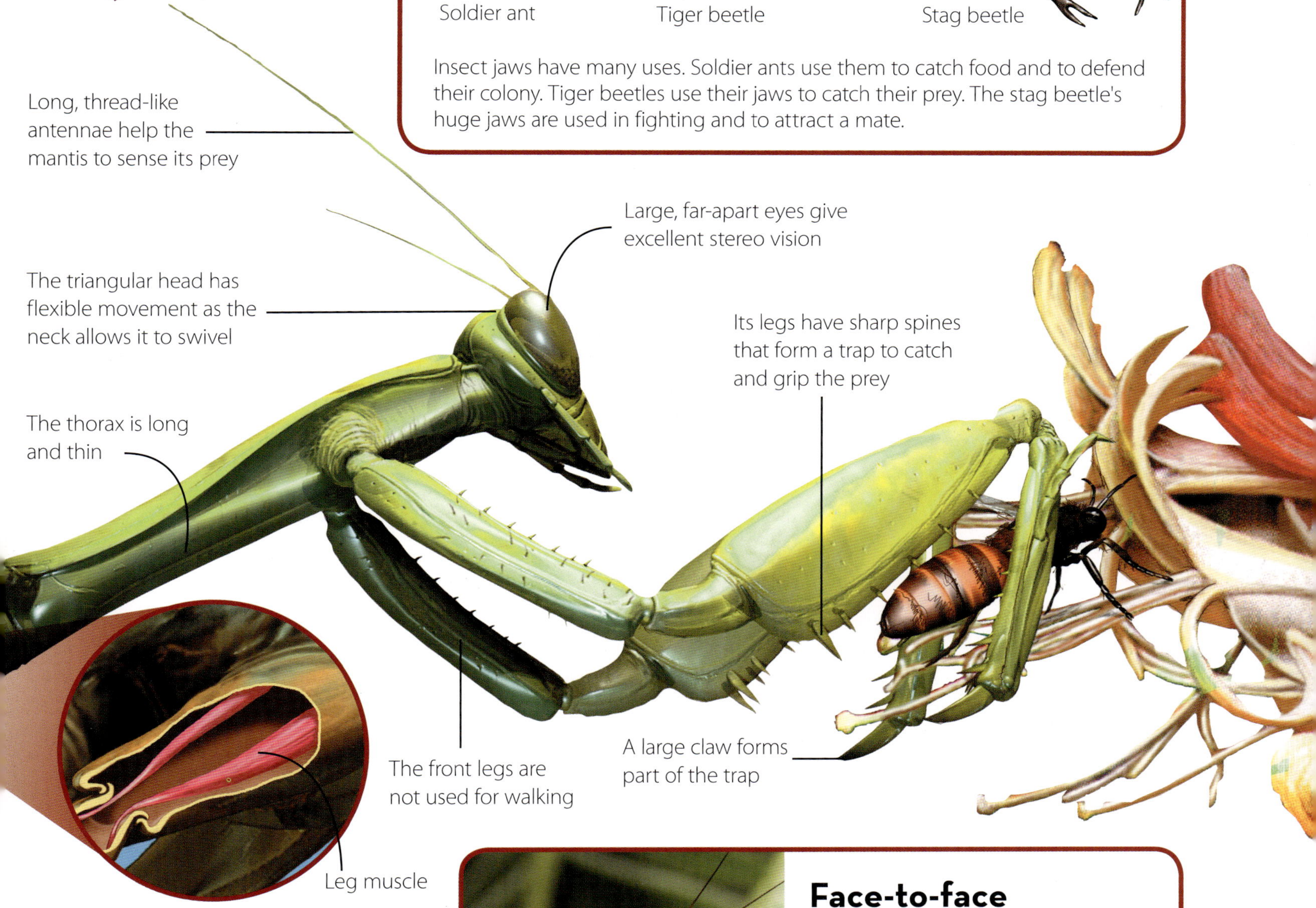

Long, thread-like antennae help the mantis to sense its prey

The triangular head has flexible movement as the neck allows it to swivel

Large, far-apart eyes give excellent stereo vision

Its legs have sharp spines that form a trap to catch and grip the prey

The thorax is long and thin

The front legs are not used for walking

A large claw forms part of the trap

Leg muscle

Leg muscles

Strong leg muscles enable the mantis to keep perfectly still until it needs to move to catch its meal. Then the leg muscles rapidly straighten. The long body of the mantis allows it to reach prey that is some distance away without having to walk or run up to it, which could give the prey time to escape.

Face-to-face

Large eyes high on a triangular head give the mantis excellent stereo (two-eyed) vision, so it can accurately judge distances. Its neck enables it to swivel its head to almost any angle. The mantis has sense organs on its neck and legs that enable it to determine exactly where to strike. Gripped in the spiny legs of the mantis, the victim is quickly passed to its mouth and sliced up by the mandibles.

Self-defence

Many animals see insects as a tasty meal, so insects have to defend themselves. Some try to avoid their enemies by using camouflage, hiding, or running or flying away but some face their predators. They may have armour that protects them – thick cuticle, a coat of spines, or poisonous hairs. Or they may be more active in their self-defence, with strong jaws to bite and stab, a painful (even deadly) sting, or the ability to produce a strong smell or loud noise that will drive a predator away. Some even secrete poisonous fluids, or, like the bombardier beetle (*right*), spray hot, irritating chemicals. Most of these masters of chemical warfare are brightly coloured so predators know to leave them alone.

Bombardier beetle

The bombardier beetle is built for speed. When it is not hunting, it lives under stones at the edges of fields. If disturbed or threatened in any way, it is well able to defend itself.

With its long antennae, the bombardier can search for prey

The beetle's large eyes are typical of an active predator

Bright coloured markings warn predators that the beetle can fight back

Long legs enable the beetle to run fast

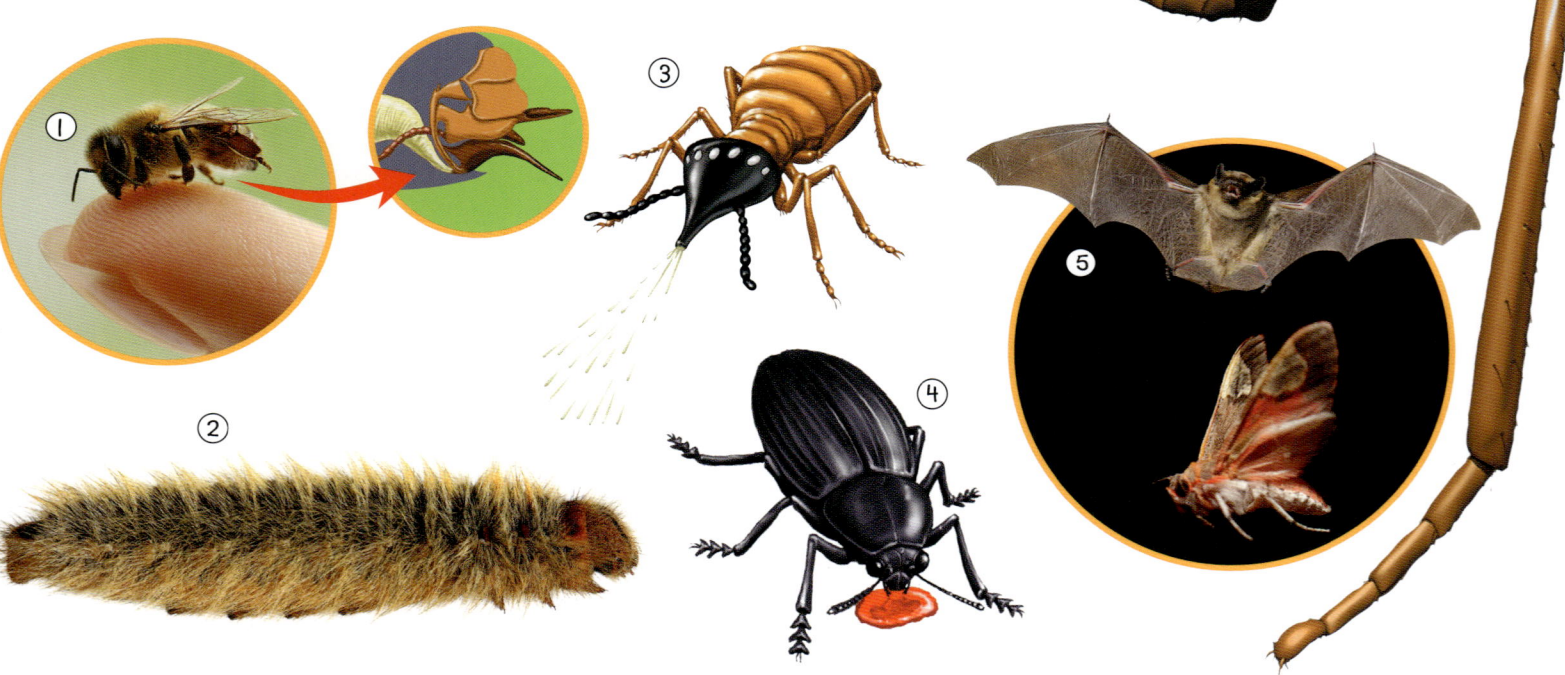

Methods of defence

Female bees (**1**) are armed with a sting. Glands in the bees produce a cocktail of irritating chemicals that can be pumped into a victim through a sharp needle-like lance. Many moth caterpillars (**2**) are covered in spines or fine hairs, which serve as protection. The hairs are sharp and break off easily, causing intense irritation in the mouth of any predator. Some termite soldiers (**3**) squirt glue at predators to defend their colony. Instead of biting, they spray a sticky substance from their glands, which entangles the predator's legs and antennae. This leaf beetle (**4**) gives off an unpleasant drop of blood from its mouth when it is alarmed, which frightens birds, its main predator. When pursued by a bat (**5**), some moths emit squeaks and clicks. A bat uses sound (echolocation) to find its prey in the dark, and the moth's noises confuse its hearing, which gives the moth a chance to escape.

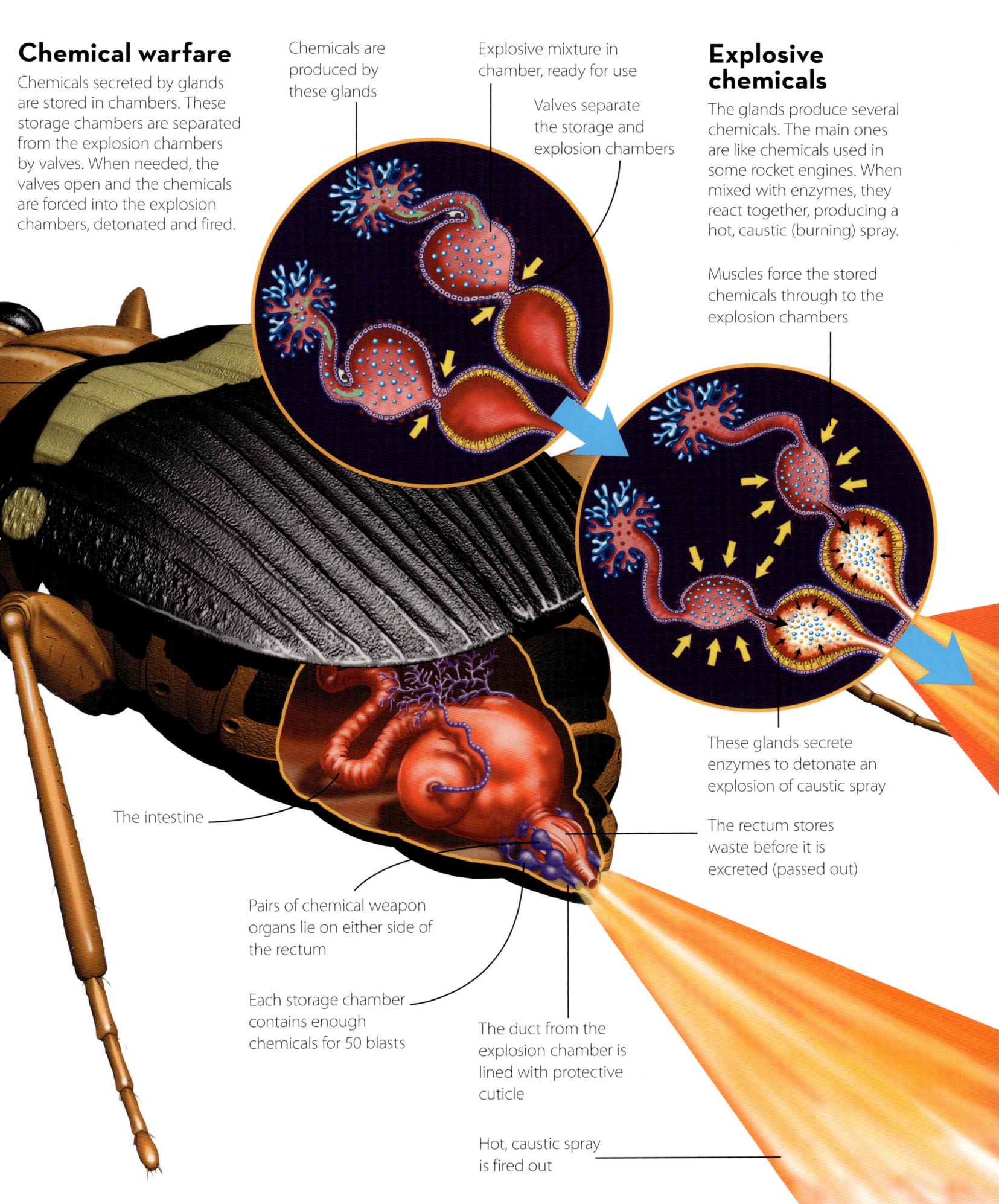

Colour and Shape

Insects are designed for survival. They come in a vast variety of colours and shapes, which help them avoid being eaten by predators. The folded wings of many butterflies are beautifully camouflaged, blending in with surrounding leaves, lichens or tree bark. When open, the wings may use colour in a different way. Vivid eye-spot markings can startle a predatory bird. Bright yellows and reds on black can signal to predators that the butterfly tastes nasty, warning them to leave it alone. So, an insect's cuticle (outer covering) can be used for disguise or, like a flag, as a signal to other animals.

The colours and patterns can be produced with pigments (colouring in the wing tissue) and by the cuticle itself. White, blues, and greens are made by the shape of the surface of the cuticle. The varying combinations of pigment and cuticle give insects their distinctive and sometimes colourful armour.

Morpho butterfly

Morpho butterflies flash blue as they fly through the sun-dappled South American rainforests, alternately exposing their colourful upper and camouflaged lower wing surfaces. The flashing attracts other morphos and confuses predators. When they are still, with their wings folded, eye spots on the wings' undersides can deter predators.

Eye spots startle predators

The wings' undersides are camouflaged to resemble dead leaves

White light shines onto the surface of the scales

Different coloured light is reflected from the ridges according to their depth

Gleaming like gold

Many beetles, such as the golden tortoise beetle, look as though they are made of metal. They owe their metallic colouring to light reflecting back off the different layers of their semi-transparent outer cuticle (1). Below this is a softer cuticle (2), beneath which is a layer of cells, glands and nerves (3).

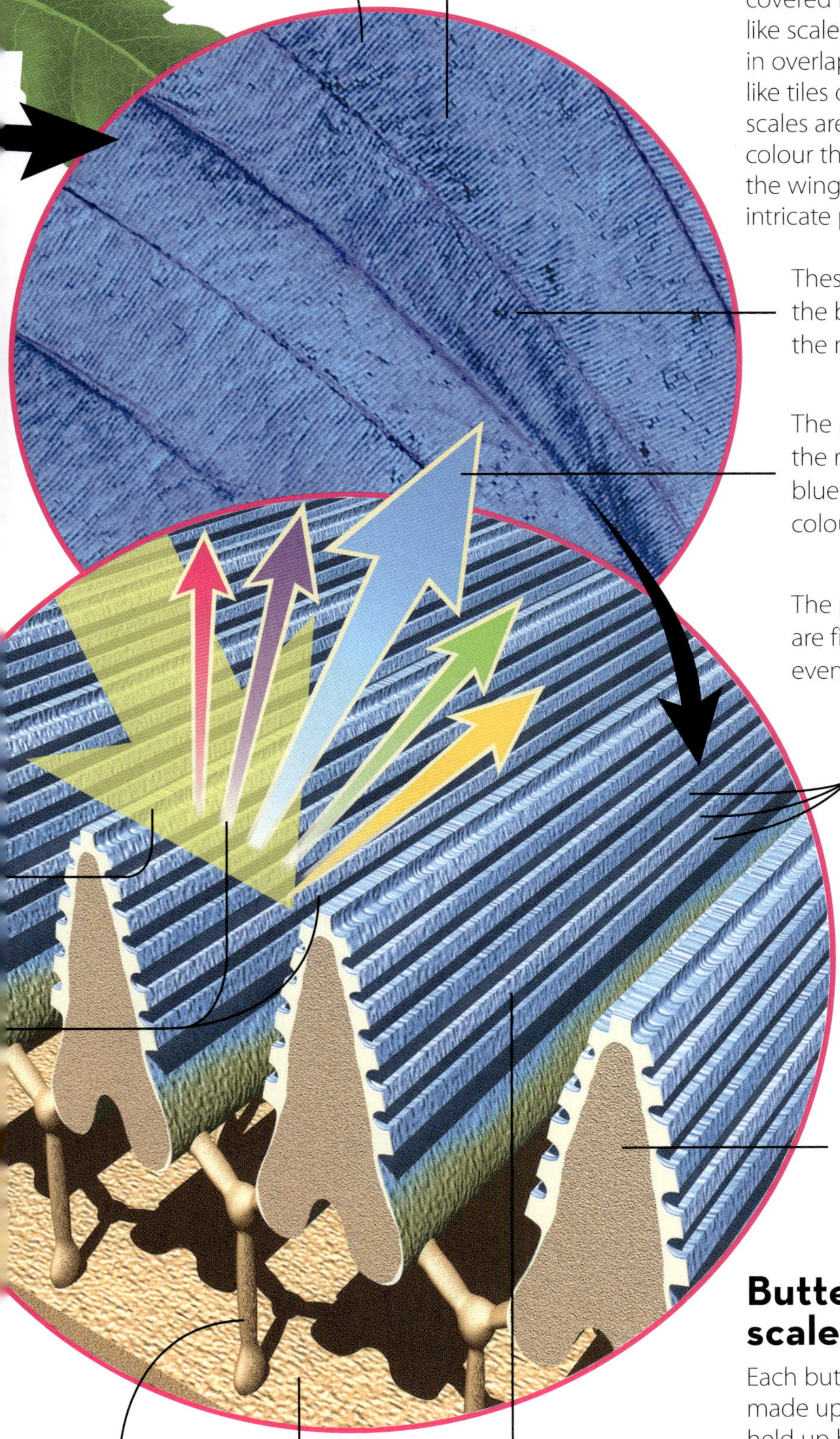

The wing of a butterfly is covered with tiny, overlapping scales

Around 7,000 of these tiny scales would cover the head of a pin

Colourful scales

A butterfly's wings are covered in thin, dust-like scales arranged in overlapping rows, like tiles on a roof. The scales are designed to colour the surface of the wing and produce intricate patterns.

These scales are from the blue upper wing of the morpho butterfly

The positions of the ridges make blue the dominant colour

The parallel ridges are fine and evenly spaced

A scale can also contain pigment that can create additional colours

Butterfly scales

Each butterfly scale is made up of parallel ridges, held up by supports. The ridges reflect each colour – blue, green and purple – in a different direction.

A Y-shaped support

The base of a scale on the butterfly's wing

Under a microscope, the ridges on a single scale are visible

Stick insects

Stick insects are aptly named. Their body, legs, and antennae are long and thin, resembling small sticks, making them very difficult to see. When they move, they are very slow.

Insect twig

Many moth caterpillars, including 'inch worms', are very thin and coloured like plants. Holding on to a twig with their rear sucker-like legs, they often extend their body out stiffly, to imitate a shoot.

Not what it seems

Some caterpillars and pupae have a strange way of disguising themselves. They pretend to be bird droppings – enough to put off any predator.

Feeding

Insects can eat almost anything! They have versatile mouthparts that can cut, lick and suck. Food is taken in through the mouth and enters the long alimentary canal, or gut, which is divided into three parts: the foregut, midgut and hindgut.

Both the foregut and the hindgut are lined with a thin layer of cuticle. The foregut begins with the oesophagus. This leads to the thorax, where it widens to form the crop. Food is stored in the crop before being passed on to the gizzard where it is ground up. The gizzard is lined with thick cuticle and spines or ridges. The midgut is not lined with cuticle, and digested food can be absorbed here. The hindgut is a coiled tube divided into three parts: the ileum, colon and rectum.

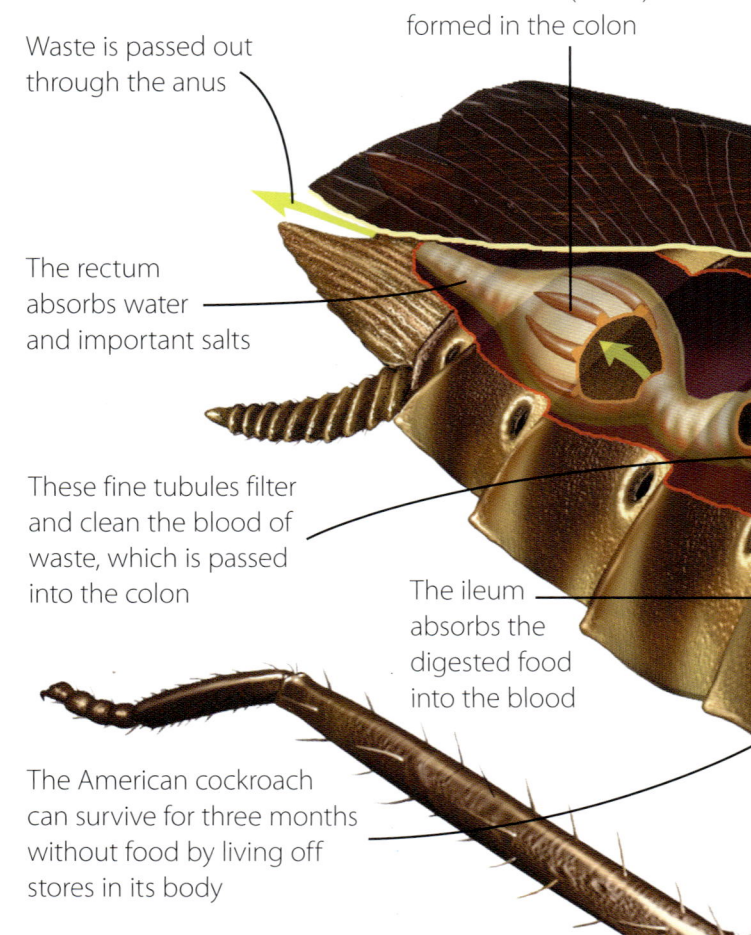

Faecal matter (waste) is formed in the colon

Waste is passed out through the anus

The rectum absorbs water and important salts

These fine tubules filter and clean the blood of waste, which is passed into the colon

The ileum absorbs the digested food into the blood

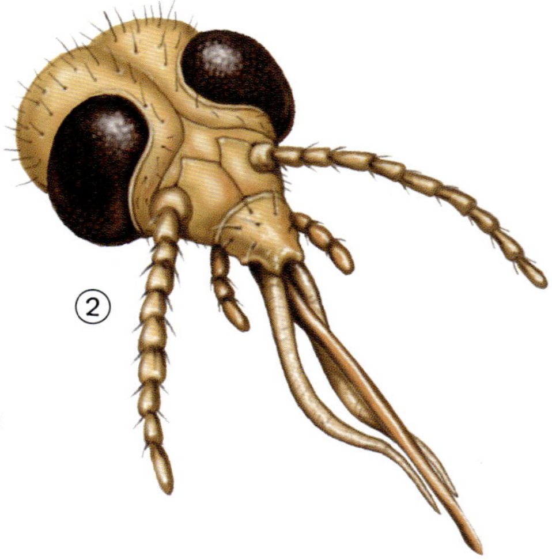

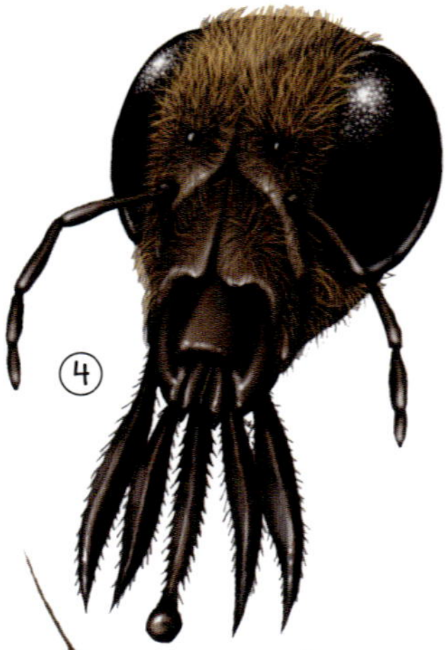

The American cockroach can survive for three months without food by living off stores in its body

Mouth parts

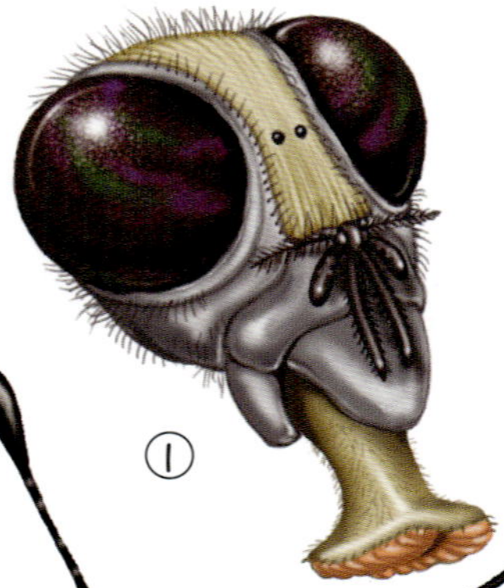

A housefly (**1**) moistens its food with saliva first, then the food and saliva are sucked up. A mosquito's mouth (**2**) consists of a tube which contains a set of cutting tools. Females pierce the skin of their prey so blood can be sucked up. Males feed on plant juices. Butterflies (**3**) have an elongated, coiled mouthpart called a proboscis, which sucks up nectar. Bees (**4**) have licking and biting mouthparts. The mandibles can bite while the tongue can lap up nectar. Bush crickets (**5**) are scavengers and hunters. They have powerful mouthparts for biting and cutting.

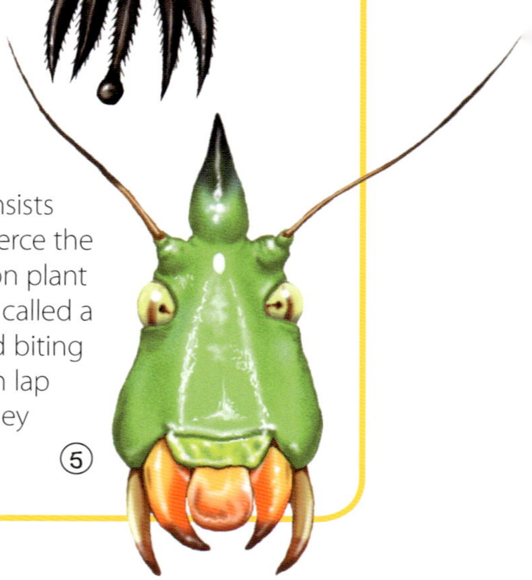

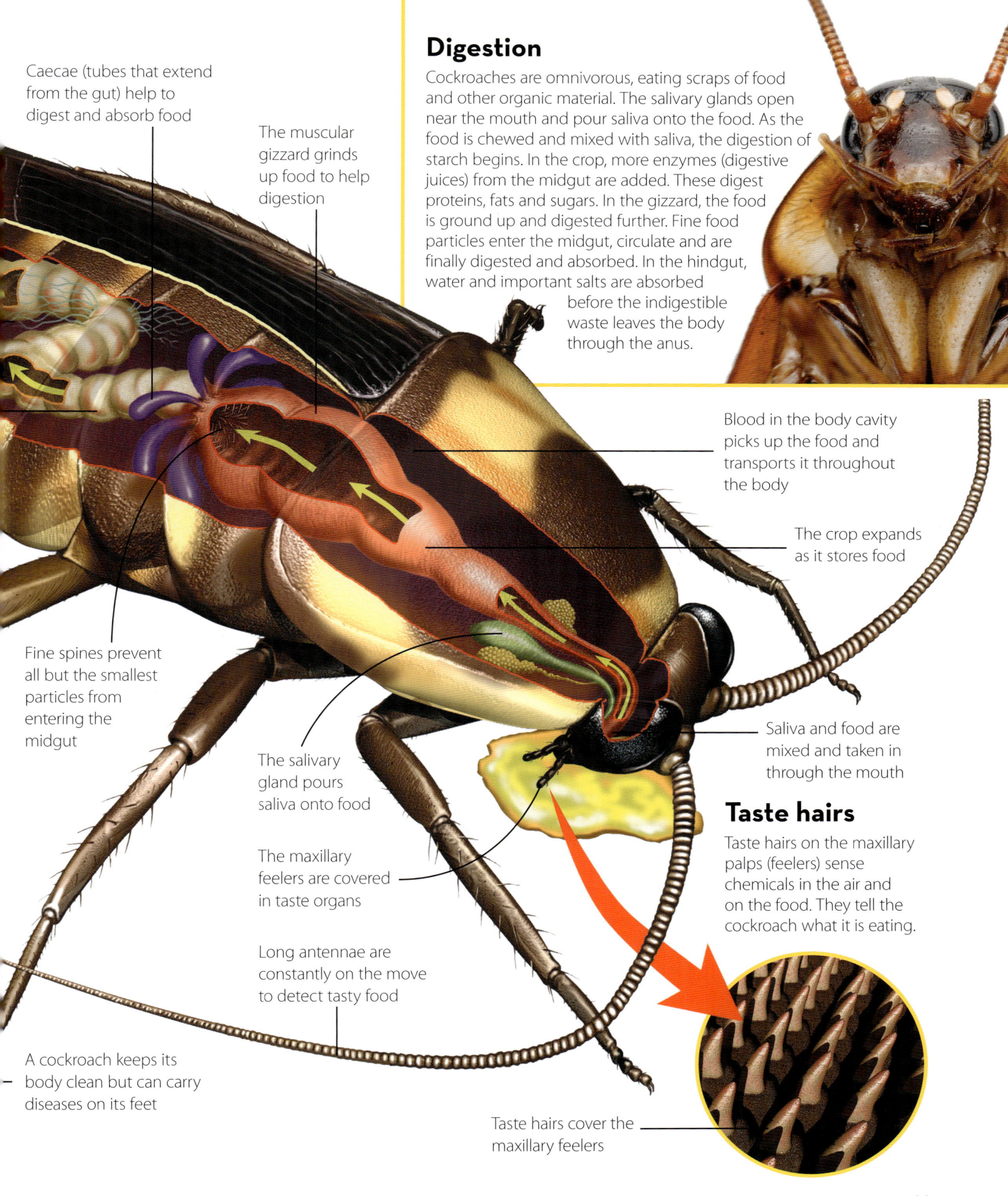

Digestion

Cockroaches are omnivorous, eating scraps of food and other organic material. The salivary glands open near the mouth and pour saliva onto the food. As the food is chewed and mixed with saliva, the digestion of starch begins. In the crop, more enzymes (digestive juices) from the midgut are added. These digest proteins, fats and sugars. In the gizzard, the food is ground up and digested further. Fine food particles enter the midgut, circulate and are finally digested and absorbed. In the hindgut, water and important salts are absorbed before the indigestible waste leaves the body through the anus.

Taste hairs

Taste hairs on the maxillary palps (feelers) sense chemicals in the air and on the food. They tell the cockroach what it is eating.

Caecae (tubes that extend from the gut) help to digest and absorb food

The muscular gizzard grinds up food to help digestion

Blood in the body cavity picks up the food and transports it throughout the body

The crop expands as it stores food

Fine spines prevent all but the smallest particles from entering the midgut

The salivary gland pours saliva onto food

Saliva and food are mixed and taken in through the mouth

The maxillary feelers are covered in taste organs

Long antennae are constantly on the move to detect tasty food

A cockroach keeps its body clean but can carry diseases on its feet

Taste hairs cover the maxillary feelers

23

Parasites

Blood from a living animal can make a tasty meal for some insects. Blood-sucking insects that live on other animals are called parasites. Their host is their food source, but living on another animal can be difficult. The host does not want them and will try to remove them. For example, to survive any attempt to be pulled or shaken off, a flea (*right*) has bristles, hairs and hooks to help it grip the host's hair. Strong claws also grip the host's skin.

A flea's exoskeleton is very thick, tough and slippery, making it hard for the host to squash or grip it. Using its powerful legs, it can jump away from danger and jump back onto its host. The flea's thin body enables it to squeeze between the host's hairs. Its mouthparts are able to penetrate the host's skin to reach the blood beneath and draw it up into the flea's expandable gut.

Digestion

Ground-up blood from the crop is squirted into the midgut and mixed with enzymes. It then moves back up to the midgut wall, where it is absorbed into the bloodstream.

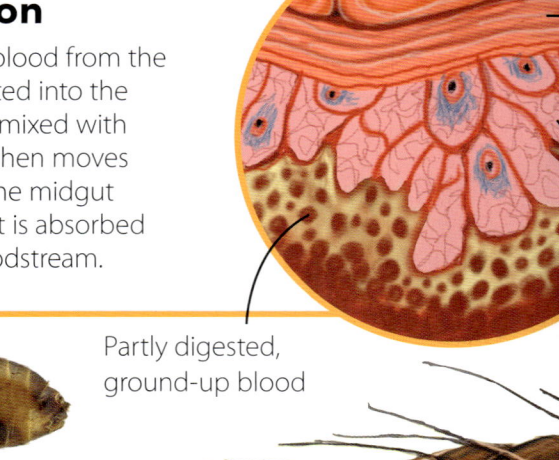

Partly digested, ground-up blood

Fleas are between 1.5 and 3 mm long – 10 to 20 times smaller than this picture

Undigested food and waste leaves through the anus

The rectum absorbs water and important salts

The vagina receives the male sex organ when mating

Sperm from the male is stored here until needed for fertilisation

After mating, the female's eggs are fertilised and sealed in eggshells in the oviduct

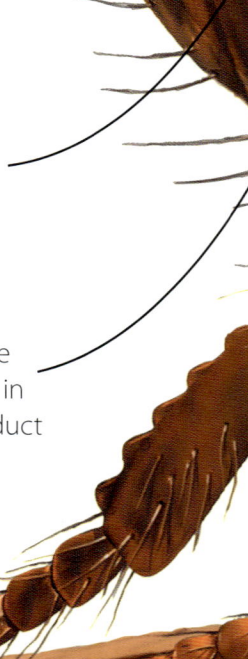

Jumping legs

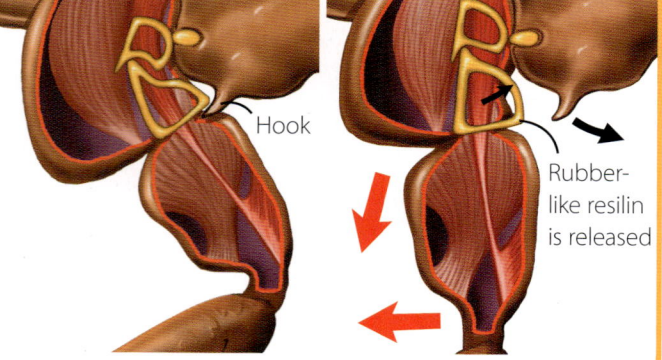

Hook

Rubber-like resilin is released

Powerful muscles pull the leg up against a hook on the flea's body, distorting a pad of rubber-like cuticle called resilin. A sideways movement of the top of the leg pulls the hook off the catch, and as the resilin pad springs back into shape (like twanging a stretched elastic band), all the stored energy from the pad is transferred to the fleas toes, catapulting it up to 40 centimetres into the air.

Muscles around the midgut move food back and forth as it is digested

Some cells in the midgut secrete digestive enzymes; others absorb digested food

Crop

Blood is pumped from the throat into the muscular crop. The crop is lined with sharp, backward-facing spines that grind up the blood cells. Valves stop the blood from being forced out of the crop until it is ready and needed. Once ground up, the contents of the crop are squeezed into the midgut for digestion.

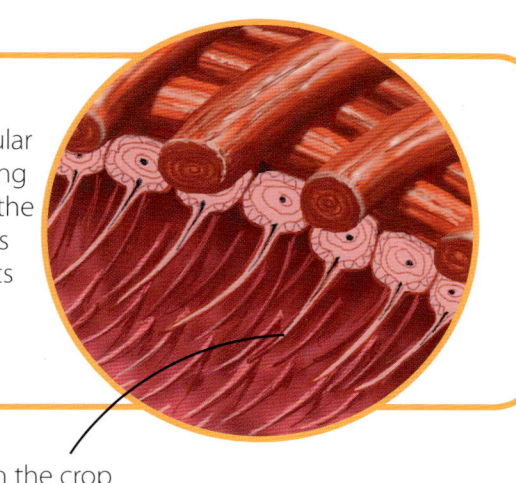

The muscular crop grinds up blood cells

The oesophagus (throat) pumps blood from the host into the crop

Short, hard spines in the crop grind up blood cells

The flat antennae can be tucked out of the way

There is a groove for each antenna

Feeding on blood

Sharp mandibles bore into the host, then saliva is forced into the wound to prevent the blood from clotting and blocking up the hole. Blood is sucked into the oesophagus, through a valve (1) and into the crop. It then passes through another valve (2) into the midgut. A valve (3) releases excess water and waste into the hindgut and rectum where water and salts are taken in. Waste stored in the rectum passes out through the anus (4).

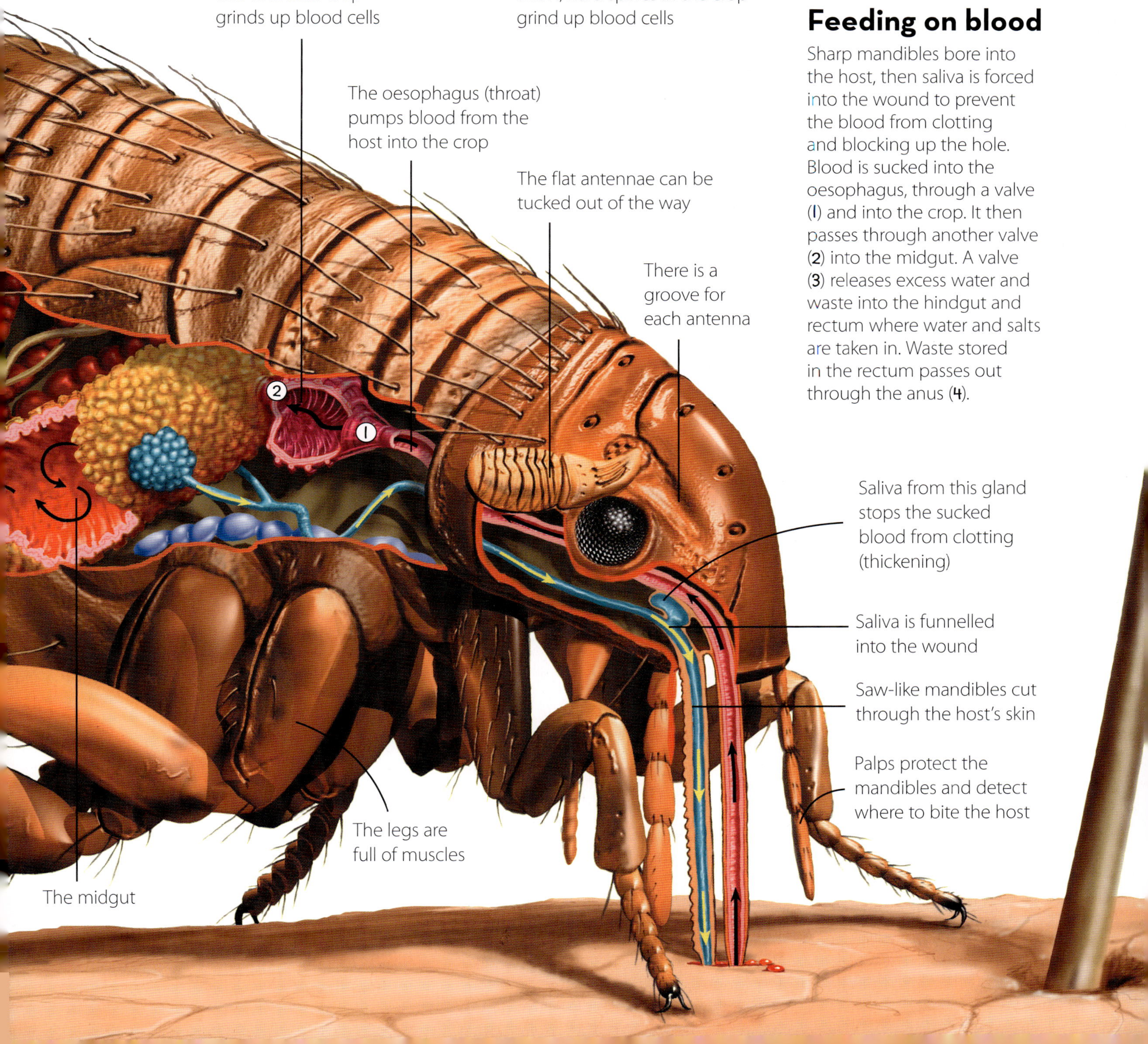

Saliva from this gland stops the sucked blood from clotting (thickening)

Saliva is funnelled into the wound

Saw-like mandibles cut through the host's skin

Palps protect the mandibles and detect where to bite the host

The legs are full of muscles

The midgut

Mating

An insect's main purpose in life is to reproduce. Some insects do not even feed, they just mate, lay eggs and die. Like most other female animals, a female insect produces eggs from a pair of ovaries. The eggs travel down to her uterus where they are fertilised by sperm produced by the male. The sperm are made in a pair of organs, called the testes, inside the male.

Some male insects leave packets of sperm on the ground for the female to pick up. However, to ensure the sperm is safe, many transfer their sperm to the female directly. The male insect climbs onto the back of the female (*right*). It then inserts its sex organ into her, to pump sperm into her uterus. The sperm may be used to fertilise eggs straight away, or stored in a sac inside the female's body until they are needed.

Fighting for territory

Rhinoceros beetles are so-named because the males are armed with 'horns'. They fight each other over the possession of a place where females they can mate with are likely to be. They try to turn each other over. The winner claims the territory and the loser leaves.

The female beetle keeps a sharp look out for predators

Ways of finding a mate

Male cicadas use sound to attract a mate. They 'sing', which brings the males together and attracts females to them. Other insects find a mate by sight. For example, female glow-worms emit light at dusk to attract a mate. And many use smell. The female moth releases tiny amounts of chemicals called pheromones, which can be detected by a male many miles away. He follows the scent to find her.

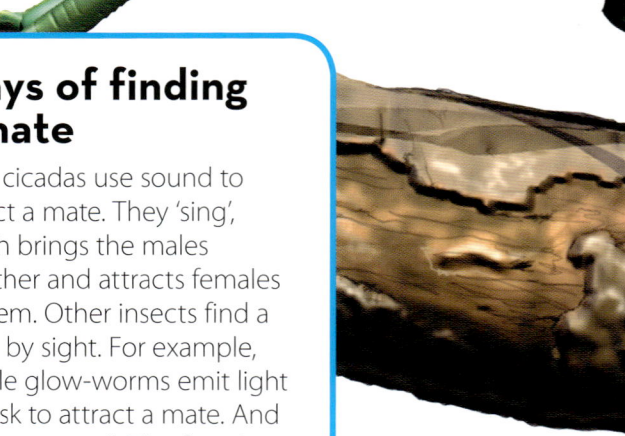

Male cicada

Female glow-worm

Female moth

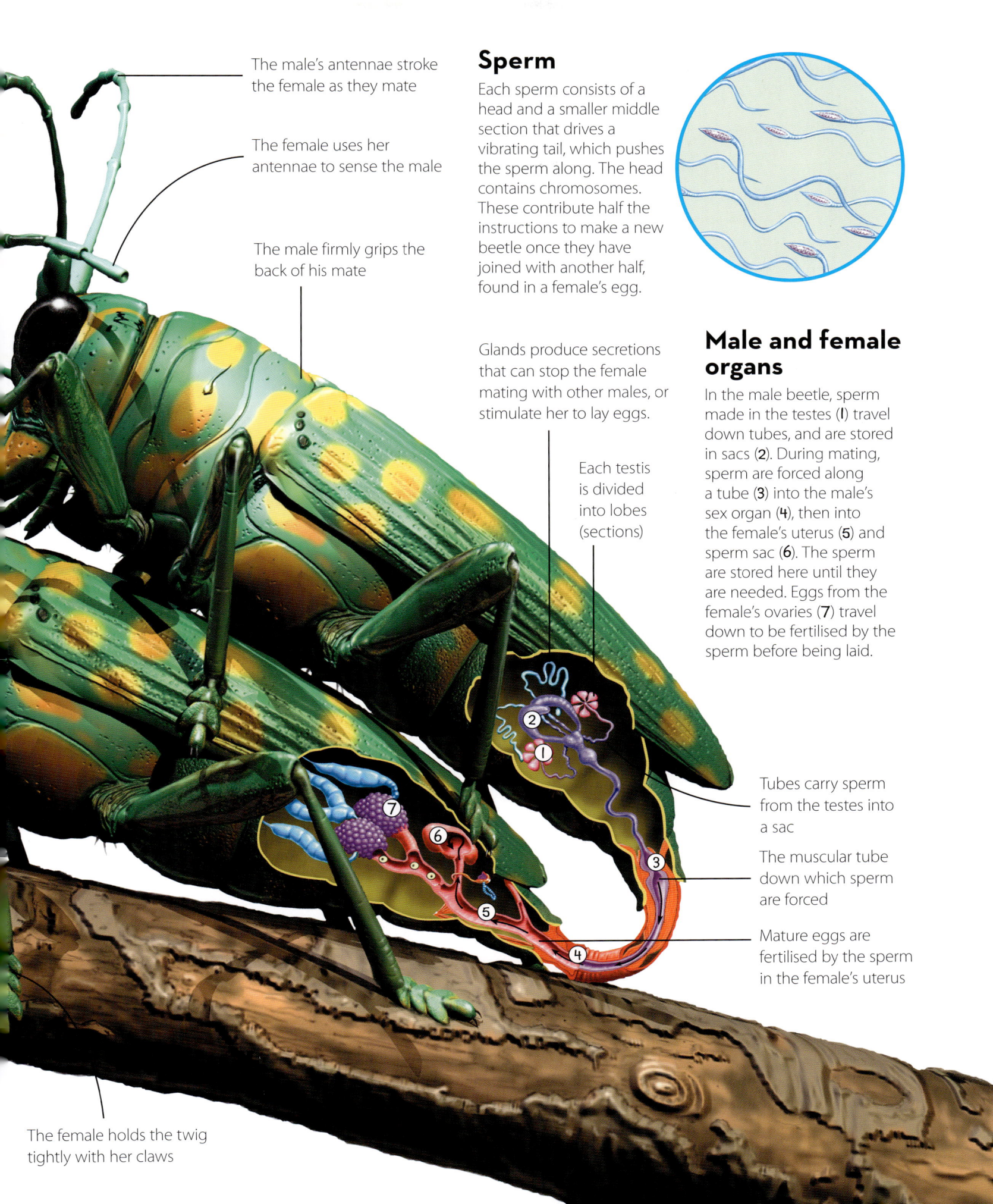

New Life

Adult insects are mainly concerned with producing their young and making sure they are safe and have plenty of food to eat. After being fertilised by a male, the female butterfly finds a place to lay her eggs – a suitable plant that will provide her offspring with food and as much protection from predators as possible.

The female then lays an egg or several eggs. Each egg is filled with a rich yolk for the developing embryo to feed on. It is tough and waterproof to seal in moisture while the egg is exposed to the air. After being laid, it may take between several days and several weeks for the embryo in the egg to develop and hatch, depending on the surrounding temperature.

A network of fine pores lets the egg breathe and keeps water in

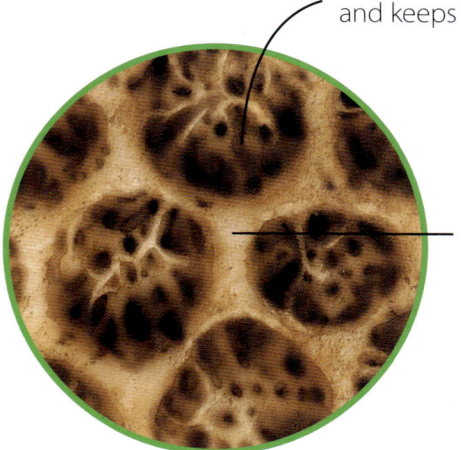

Rigid supports are connected to columns beneath

Eggshell structure

Through a microscope, we can see complicated patterns of pores on the surface of the eggshell. These lead into cavities, which let the egg breathe without losing precious moisture. Many insect eggs allow the developing embryo to breathe in both wet and dry conditions, in case the egg is covered by a raindrop.

Laying eggs

Each egg consists of a cell that will join with the sperm and grow, and a ball of cells that surround the yolk. The yolk is the developing insect's source of food. Cells in the ovary produce the surrounding eggshell. Before the egg is laid, sperm that has been stored in a pouch enters the egg through a special pore in the eggshell. The female also produces a gluey substance to stick the egg to the plant's surface.

Each ovary produces oocytes rich in yolk

The oocytes grow and develop into a ball of cells

The eggs are fertilised by stored sperm from the male

Special glands help the egg-laying process

The breathing area of the egg is protected by a hollow

The laid eggs are stuck firmly to a plant

When the eggs hatch, the plant will be a food source for the young caterpillars

All sorts of eggs

Lacewing eggs (**1**) are suspended on the ends of fine threads away from predators. Butterflies glue their tiny, flask-shaped eggs (**2**) to plants. Cockroaches lay eight eggs in tough packets called oothecae (**3**). Stick insects' eggs (**4**) have a lid that pops open to release the young, and water scorpions' eggs (**5**) have breathing horns that poke above the surface of the water. For safety, some sawflies lay their eggs (**6**) inside leaves close to the veins.

Before fertilisation, the egg is called an oocyte

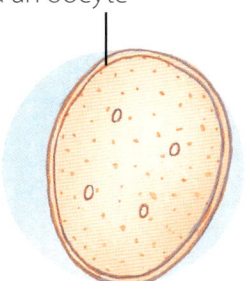

A ball of cells surrounds the yolk

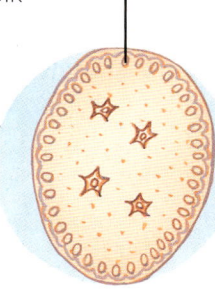

Once fertilised, the egg is called a zygote

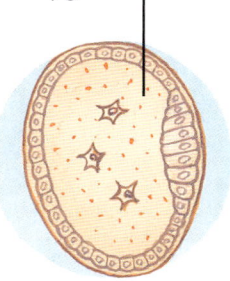

The developing embryo shows an insect shape

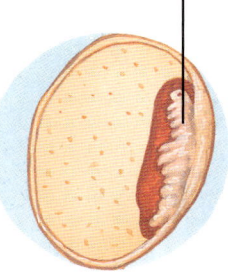

Embryo development

Some insects have a three-stage life cycle and some go through five stages, but all insects begin life as an egg. Before fertilisation, the egg cell divides to form a sphere of cells called an oocyte, with some scattered cells drifting in the yolk. The cells continue to divide. The eggshell is produced by the outer cells. One cell is fertilised by the sperm from the male and the egg is laid. The fertilised cell, called a zygote, divides and forms the embryo, which will develop into the young insect. At this stage, the beginnings of the mouthparts, antennae and legs can just be seen. Once developed, the egg hatches and either a larva (in a five-stage life cycle) or a nymph (*see page 30*) will crawl out.

Changing Shape

Many insects hatch from eggs as nymphs, which moult (shed their outer skin) and gradually grow to their adult size. But others, such as butterflies, undergo a total metamorphosis (change) and hatch once from their egg, and a second time from their pupa.

A butterfly's first stage of life is in caterpillar form. Its soft cuticle (outer skin) allows its body to expand as it eats and grows. When the cuticle becomes too tight, it is cast off and a new one forms as the caterpillar continues to get larger. After a few weeks, the caterpillar changes into a chrysalis, or pupa. This is known as the pupal stage. About a month later, the adult butterfly hatches, ready to find a mate and produce more butterflies.

8) New butterfly

Immediately after breaking out, the new butterfly has to stretch and expand its wings by pumping blood into the wing veins. The expanded wings then dry out and the butterfly uses them to soar into the air.

7) Emergence

About a month after the chrysalis was formed, and the process of change is complete, the adult butterfly emerges from its chrysalis. Puffing itself up with air causes the case to split open, allowing the butterfly to crawl free.

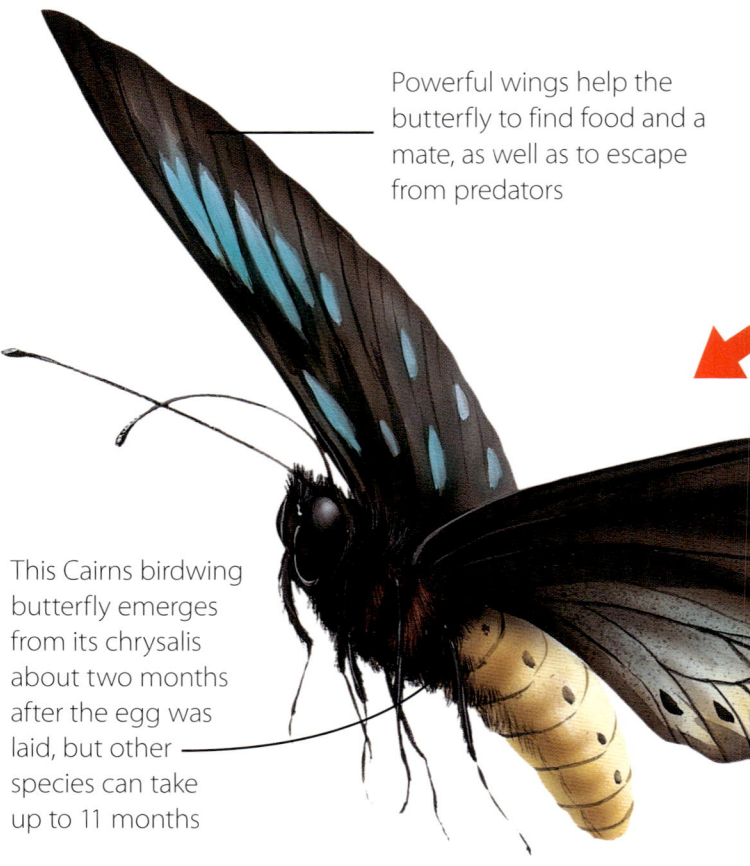

Powerful wings help the butterfly to find food and a mate, as well as to escape from predators

This Cairns birdwing butterfly emerges from its chrysalis about two months after the egg was laid, but other species can take up to 11 months

1) Eggs

The female butterfly lays clusters of eggs on a plant, which will provide food for the caterpillars after they hatch. The eggshells stick to the leaf and keep the developing caterpillars from drying out.

Air passes through special holes in the tops of the eggs

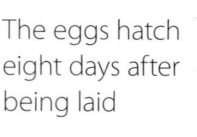

2) Hatching

All the eggs hatch at the same time. The young caterpillar bites a hole in the top of the eggshell, then it crawls out and eats the shell before starting to eat the plant.

The eggs hatch eight days after being laid

A caterpillar sheds its skin (moults) several times as it grows bigger

A larger, soft new skin enables further growth

Old skin

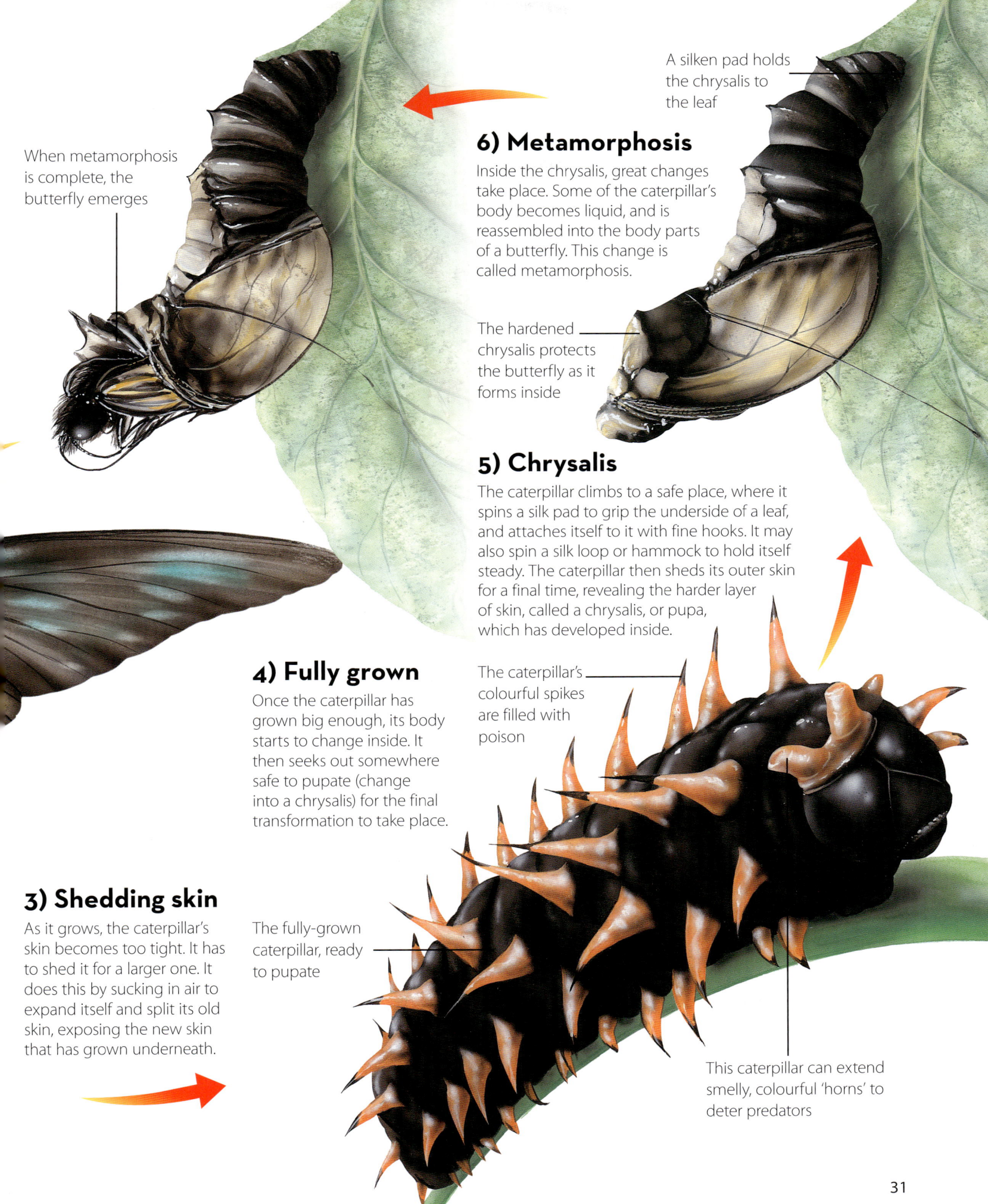

When metamorphosis is complete, the butterfly emerges

A silken pad holds the chrysalis to the leaf

6) Metamorphosis

Inside the chrysalis, great changes take place. Some of the caterpillar's body becomes liquid, and is reassembled into the body parts of a butterfly. This change is called metamorphosis.

The hardened chrysalis protects the butterfly as it forms inside

5) Chrysalis

The caterpillar climbs to a safe place, where it spins a silk pad to grip the underside of a leaf, and attaches itself to it with fine hooks. It may also spin a silk loop or hammock to hold itself steady. The caterpillar then sheds its outer skin for a final time, revealing the harder layer of skin, called a chrysalis, or pupa, which has developed inside.

4) Fully grown

Once the caterpillar has grown big enough, its body starts to change inside. It then seeks out somewhere safe to pupate (change into a chrysalis) for the final transformation to take place.

The caterpillar's colourful spikes are filled with poison

3) Shedding skin

As it grows, the caterpillar's skin becomes too tight. It has to shed it for a larger one. It does this by sucking in air to expand itself and split its old skin, exposing the new skin that has grown underneath.

The fully-grown caterpillar, ready to pupate

This caterpillar can extend smelly, colourful 'horns' to deter predators

31

Ant Nest

Ants live together in complex societies. There are over 5,000 different kinds of ant community. Each nest is headed by a queen that is cared for by female workers. Some ants have different types of workers, called castes, which do different tasks. Ants build their nests in all kinds of places. Here, the nest is both above and below the ground. Workers burrow in the soil and pile up the material they dig out on the surface above. The mound itself is then dug with tunnels and chambers too, which connect with the ones below ground. In this maze, the queen ant lives, the eggs and larvae are cared for, and food is stored. At certain times, winged queens and males are produced. These leave the nest in mass swarms several times every summer to mate.

Egg-laying queen

The queen is much larger than her workers. She is the only ant in the nest that lays eggs. As the eggs are laid, they are looked after by attendant workers. On hatching, the young larvae are moved to other chambers where they become pupae (chrysalises). Ants will emerge from the pupae.

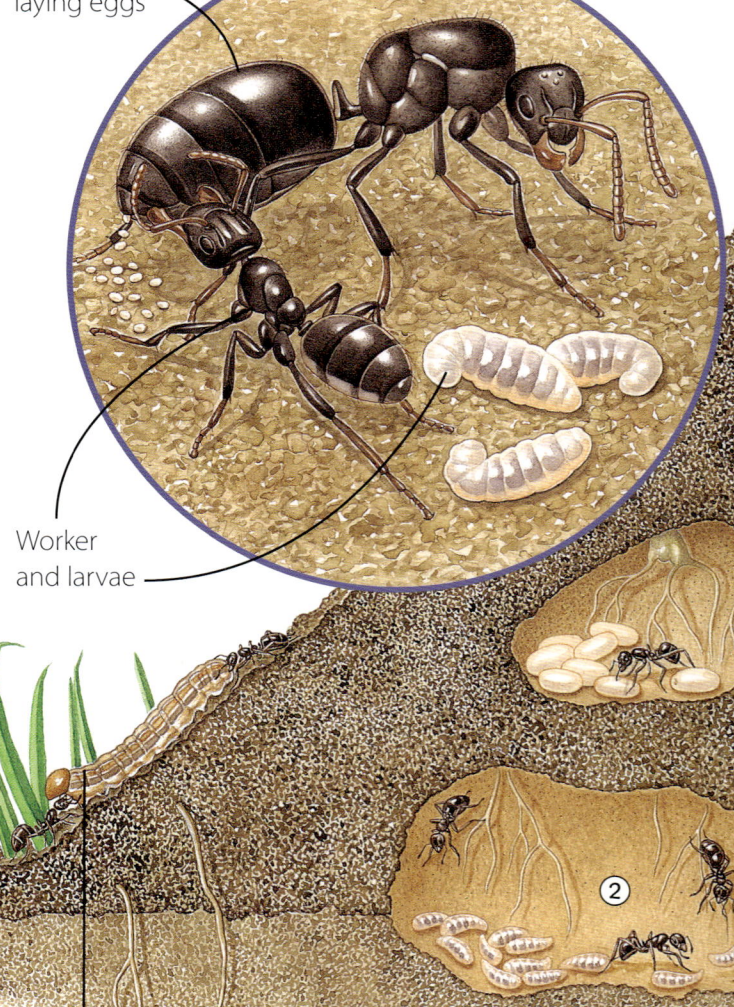

Queen, laying eggs

Worker and larvae

A caterpillar is dragged back to the nest for food

A worker ant collecting honeydew from an aphid

Secretions from the workers prevent the eggs and larvae from going mouldy

Queen's chamber with the egg-laying queen, and workers tending the eggs and larvae

Herding aphids

To feed, tiny insects called aphids suck plant sap. This sap contains a lot of water and sugar, far more than the aphids need, so they pass out the excess. Ants have a very sweet tooth and collect this sugary liquid, which is called honeydew. To make the aphids produce more, the ants direct aphids to the juiciest parts of plants, and stroke their backs. The ants also look after the aphids, guarding them from predators.

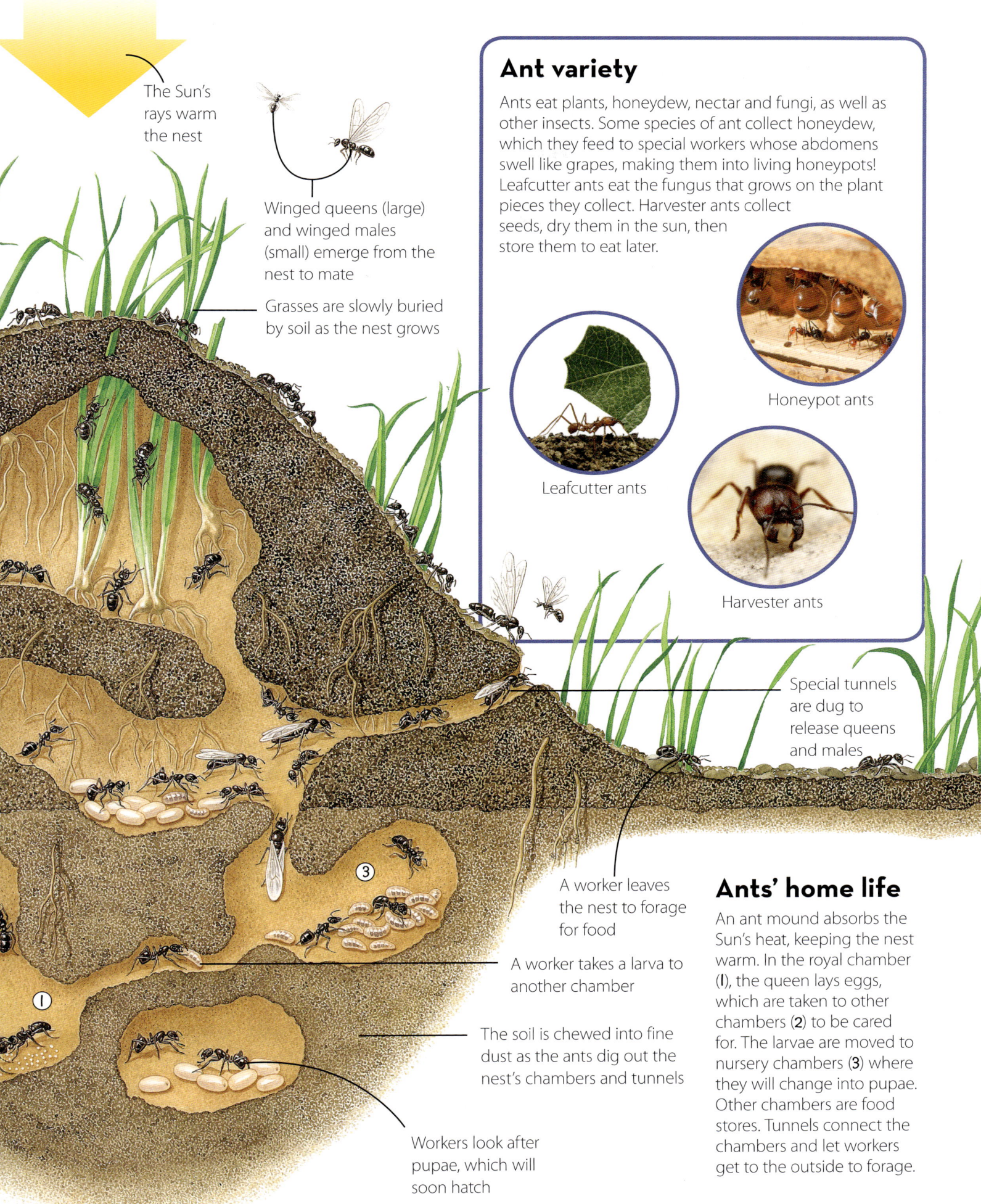

The Sun's rays warm the nest

Winged queens (large) and winged males (small) emerge from the nest to mate

Grasses are slowly buried by soil as the nest grows

Ant variety

Ants eat plants, honeydew, nectar and fungi, as well as other insects. Some species of ant collect honeydew, which they feed to special workers whose abdomens swell like grapes, making them into living honeypots! Leafcutter ants eat the fungus that grows on the plant pieces they collect. Harvester ants collect seeds, dry them in the sun, then store them to eat later.

Leafcutter ants

Honeypot ants

Harvester ants

Special tunnels are dug to release queens and males

A worker leaves the nest to forage for food

A worker takes a larva to another chamber

The soil is chewed into fine dust as the ants dig out the nest's chambers and tunnels

Workers look after pupae, which will soon hatch

Ants' home life

An ant mound absorbs the Sun's heat, keeping the nest warm. In the royal chamber (1), the queen lays eggs, which are taken to other chambers (2) to be cared for. The larvae are moved to nursery chambers (3) where they will change into pupae. Other chambers are food stores. Tunnels connect the chambers and let workers get to the outside to forage.

Bee Nest

Honey bee nests are busy places. In each nest, a bustling community of up to 60,000 insects live together. Nearly all the bees are females, called workers, which hatch from fertilised eggs laid by the queen that is in charge of the colony. Only males (known as drones) hatch from unfertilised eggs. They appear in the summer and autumn. They do not work, as their only job is to mate with new queens.

All the worker bees live together, building and looking after their home, collecting food and water, feeding the young and caring for the queen. They secrete wax to make their nest. Sheets of strong, hexagonal cells hang down and hold the eggs, larvae, nectar (which becomes honey) and pollen. Being able to store food allows honey bees to live through times when food is scarce, such as in winter.

A drone (male bee) has large eyes for finding young queens to mate with

An inner crescent of cells is filled with pollen, a protein-rich food

The outer cells are filled with nectar, which is turned into honey by the bees; the cell is then sealed

A worker bee, called a forager, brings back pollen to feed the young

A forager sets off in search of pollen, nectar, water, or any other item the colony may need

Bees communicate with each other by passing food and chemicals from the queen

A worker bee may travel 2.5 kilometres to find nectar

Building cells

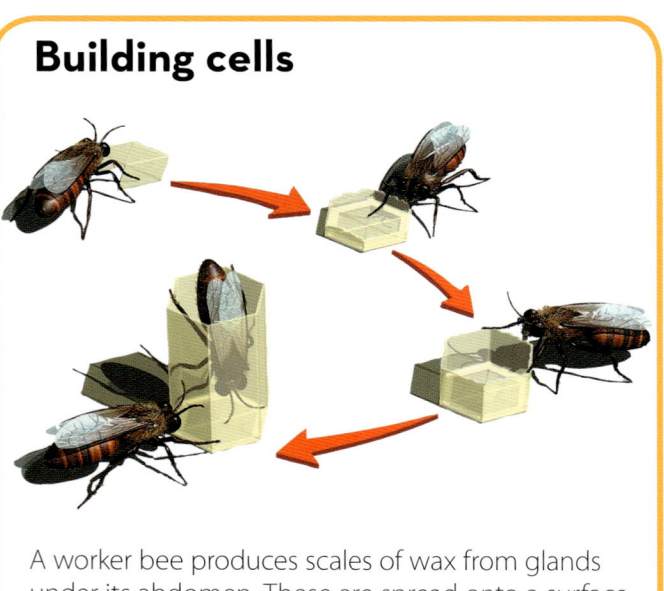

A worker bee produces scales of wax from glands under its abdomen. These are spread onto a surface using its jaws. More wax is added and shaped into a hexagonal cell. Cells are produced together, forming a sheet of honeycomb with cells on both sides, each angled slightly upwards. Combs of these cells hang side by side, just close enough to allow two bees to pass each other.

A layer of wax on a twig supports the downward-hanging comb

A honey-filled cell provides a store of food

A cell that has been filled with pollen

Queen

A queen can lay over 2,000 eggs a day. At certain times, some of these are laid in special large cells. Larvae from these eggs get extra food and grow into young queens. When they are about to hatch, the old queen leaves the nest with the older workers. This 'swarm' sets up home elsewhere and the new queen takes over the old nest.

After about six days, the cell is capped with wax by a worker bee, and the larva spins a cocoon around itself

A nurse bee cleans cells and looks after the brood

The cap is off this cell – the fifteen-day-old pupa inside will soon hatch

After about 3 days, the egg hatches into a larva. Larvae are fed on special food, called royal jelly, for a few days, then on honey and pollen

The queen lays a single egg in each cell. Fertilised eggs grow into workers, unfertilised ones into drones

A pollen load is packed into a 'basket' on the bee's back leg

A special large cell on the edge of the comb contains a developing queen bee

Waggle dance

A bee can tell other bees where it has found a lot of food by dancing. The angle it dances at tells the other bees which direction to go in to find it. The faster the bee waggles, the more food there is. The number of turns she makes in a given time indicates the distance they must go.

Rainforest Life

Tropical heat and moisture are ideal for the growth of rainforests. Here, insects are the most numerous and varied form of animal life. Nearly 200 species of butterfly can be found in a single hectare of South East Asian rainforest. However, we do not know how many rainforest insects there are in total – there may still be millions to discover.

Insects can be difficult to see as many fly high in the treetops, and many are so well camouflaged that they look just like a flower, thorn or leaf. Others live hidden inside rotting wood, living plants or leaves. Insects are a very important part of forest life – they pollinate plants and help to recycle waste matter into reusable nutrients.

Mantis

This is not a pretty flower, but a dangerous predator! Disguised to match the flower upon which it sits, this mantis waits patiently for an insect to visit the flower – then it will pounce.

Mantis

These tree hoppers can suck plant sap in safety – they are disguised as thorns, hence their other name: thornbugs

Poisonous spines on caterpillars stop predators from thinking they are an easy meal

Grasshoppers

Powerful back legs allow grasshoppers to jump out of the way of danger. These green nymphs are well camouflaged and difficult to see in the forest.

Grasshopper nymphs (young)

Leafcutter ants

Strong leafcutter ants cut pieces of leaves and carry them to their nest. They eat the fungus that begins to grow on the leaf pieces.

A leafcutter ant carrying a piece of leaf back to its nest

Not a dead leaf but a leaf insect

Insects in Water

Many types of insect live in fresh water at some time in their lives. Several, including flies such as the dragonfly as well as true flies, only spend the earliest part of their lives there – as nymphs (young that resemble the adult insect) or larvae (a worm-like form that does not resemble the adult until later on).

Other freshwater insects, like beetles and bugs, live in water both during their early and adult stages. The adults also live on land, travelling through the air to new habitats. Because large amounts of dissolved oxygen can be found in water, many insects are able to breathe in it. Most nymphs use gills to breathe, but other insects breathe at the water's surface. A few take a pocket of air down with them when they dive, returning to the surface to get more when the oxygen runs out. Insects use their legs and even their wings to swim about.

A mayfly's life

Mayfly nymphs feed on dead vegetation and live in tubes in mud or crawl amongst aquatic plants. As adults, they have just a day to live. During that time, they do not eat but only mate and lay eggs.

A mayfly

Whirligig beetles spin around on the surface looking for food

Mosquito larvae and pupae breathe through the surface film of the water

Air is trapped under the great diving beetle's wing covers

Its legs push against the water, forcing the beetle forward

It has broad, oar-like back legs for swimming

Great diving beetle

During adulthood and as larvae, these beetles are fast, aggressive predators. Adults are sleek and smooth, and have broad oar-like back legs, fringed with bristles for rapid swimming. Their front legs are adapted to grasping their prey. When they are under water, they breathe using air trapped in hairs beneath their wing covers.

The diving beetle's strong front legs can grasp prey

An adult dragonfly catches its prey using basket-like spiny front legs

Life cycle of a dragonfly

The dragonfly lays its eggs underwater, in or on water plants. The eggs hatch as predatory nymphs (1). As each nymph grows, it moults and gradually changes. Eventually it crawls out of the water (2) and emerges as an adult dragonfly with tiny wings (3), which it inflates and dries before flying off in search of food or a mate (4).

Life on the surface

The surface of the water, known as the surface film, is home to several insect hunters and scavengers. Tiny wingless springtails called Podura (5) scavenge for food. Aptly-named pond skaters (6) are fast hunters, but they will also take trapped and drowned prey. The water boatman (7) hangs from the surface of the water waiting for prey. Using its powerful legs, it chases its victim, killing it with its stabbing mouthparts.

A dragonfly nymph catches a tadpole using its 'mask'

Fly larvae feed on debris at the bottom of ponds

'Masked' hunter

A dragonfly nymph catches its prey using a special mouthpart, known as a 'mask'. The mask stays folded under the head (*top*) until the nymph shoots it forward (*bottom*) and catches the prey using the strong jaws at its tip.

A mayfly nymph scurries along the pond floor looking for food

The caddisfly larva makes a home of stones or plant remains

Woodland Life

Trees make perfect homes for many insects, providing plenty of food and places to shelter. One tree in particular, the oak, supports a huge variety of insect life, including over 210 species of moths and butterflies. Insects make use of all the tree – from the leaves, shoots and flowers in the canopy to the roots underground. They chew the leaves from the outside and inside, burrow under the bark and into the wood, and live inside the tree's fruits, acorns. As well as eating the tree, they also use it as a refuge, hiding in crevices in the bark.

Some insects are parasites, living on the insects that feed on the plant. Others are predators, searching and hunting for prey. Throughout the year, different insects can be found on different parts of every tree in a woodland.

Marble gall
Gall wasps have two types of larvae. Those of one species produce marble galls on one type of oak and bud-galls on another.

Purple hairstreak
This butterfly only lives on oak. Its caterpillars feed at night on young leaves. When fully grown they pupate in the soil. If taken into an ant nest they are better protected from predators.

Oak bark beetle
Just below the bark a female beetle makes a tunnel where she lays her eggs. The grubs that hatch make long vertical tunnels as they feed.

Acorn weevil
Like all nut weevils, the acorn weevil has a long, thin snout. At its tip are mandibles, which it uses to pierce a hole and bore into the acorn. Here it lays an egg, and the grub (larva) feeds in its ready-made larder. When the acorn falls, the grub comes out and develops into a pupa in the soil.

Lacewing
Delicate lacewings are active in the evening. Both adults and larvae hunt aphids. The larvae camouflage themselves by sticking pieces of debris to their back, including the dried husks of their prey.

Thorn moth
Adult moths are well camouflaged – their brown, jagged wings look like dead leaves. If a thorn moth caterpillar is disturbed or at rest, it makes itself look (very convincingly) like a twig.

Oak sawfly
Sawflies are related to bees and wasps. Their larvae are slug-like caterpillars. Oak sawfly caterpillars produce blistering marks as they feed on the underside of the leaf.

Lobster moth
When resting, the lobster moth caterpillar has a strange appearance, hence its name. Although it eats oak leaves it will also eat the leaves of other trees.

Seven-spotted ladybird
Most ladybirds are predators. As larvae and adults they eat huge numbers of sap-sucking aphids. Their bright colours warn predators that they taste nasty and so should not be eaten.

Dark crimson underwing moth
When at rest, with its wings folded, this moth is perfectly camouflaged on the oak tree's bark. Its caterpillars eat oak buds and pupate amongst the lichen on the tree trunk.

Types of gall
Some insects and larvae inject small amounts of chemicals into trees. The trees then produce balls of thickened tissue called galls, that limit the damage to the tree, and provide food and shelter for the larvae. Different species of gall wasp produce different types of galls, such as curved leaf galls (1), cotton-wool galls (2), spangle galls (3), and oak apples (4).

Desert Insects

Deserts are mainly hot and dry, having little rainfall, so the environment is a difficult one for animals to survive in. Those that do are specially adapted to the harsh conditions. Many hide away during the extreme heat of the day, either under rocks, or buried in the sand or deep in burrows.

Only at night and early morning, when it is cool, do they emerge to feed. Those insects that do come out during the day move from place to place quickly, keeping in the shade. Their feet are often specially adapted so that they are able to touch the hot sand when necessary, and they have a thick cuticle to reduce the loss of moisture. Some gather moisture to drink in the early morning mist, while others rely on the moisture in their food to sustain them. Even if they do lose water they can withstand a great deal of dehydration (water loss).

Dune cricket

The dune cricket (**3**) uses its flower-shaped feet to dig in the sand to escape predators and the heat of the Sun. When the temperature falls, the cricket emerges to feed on the sparse vegetation.

Tiger beetle

Like a tiger in the jungle, a tiger beetle (**4**) hunts its prey. These agile and fast predators have powerful jaws to kill even quite large insects.

Head-stander

Water droplets from early morning mist condense on this darkling beetle (**5**). It stands on tiptoe so the droplets run together and down to its mouth.

Hunting wasp

A hunting wasp lives a solitary life. A female (**1**) digs a burrow and then hunts for insects. Using her sting she paralyses her prey and takes it back to the burrow. Here she lays an egg on it. The larva that hatches feeds on the living victim.

Harvester ants

Harvester ants (**2**) nest underground, away from the Sun's intense heat. Foragers gather seeds for food which they first dry in the Sun before storing them in special chambers inside their nest. They eat the seeds as needed. They also eat insects such as caterpillars.

Deep underground, the nest chambers are cool

Ant lion

At the bottom of its pit, an ant lion (**6**) flicks sand at an ant, making it slip down into the ant lion's jaws.

Eburnea beetle

Most darkling beetles are black, so this one is unusual in being white (**7**). Darkling beetles form a large part of the desert fauna. Their hard, thick armour protects them from desiccation (drying up).

Long-legged beetle

Extra long legs allow this darkling beetle (**8**) to move fast and keep its body well clear of the hot desert sand. Moisture gathers on its back in the early morning.

Jewel wasp

Flying insects, such as the jewel wasp (*above*), need a lot of fuel to work their wings. They get this from nectar produced by desert flowers. In return, the plant is pollinated.

Laying eggs

Locusts (**9**) produce their eggs in batches inside tough, waterproof packages called oothecae. Using a special egg-laying tube, a female deposits these beneath the surface of the sand away from predators.

Flying locusts can travel thousands of kilometres in search of food

Darkling beetle

Most species of darkling beetles are a dull black (**12**), but their body shape can differ greatly. The majority are nocturnal scavengers that feed largely on plant remains.

Dung beetle

Dung beetles (**11**) gather dung into balls, roll it to safety and bury it. Underground, they lay their eggs on the dung so the larvae that hatch have a plentiful food source.

Desert grasshopper

Is it a stone? No, it's a desert grasshopper (**10**). These grasshoppers live wherever there is sufficient plant life. To avoid being eaten, they are well-camouflaged to resemble the stones of the surrounding desert.

Microscopic Life

Hidden away in their secret worlds are thousands of microscopic insects. Insects are the most successful group of living animals on Earth partly because many of them make use of the tiniest of spaces – including the gaps between grains of cereal, in the crevices in tree bark and in the fur of mammals.

Within most groups of insects there are species that are microscopic. Despite their tiny size, they have the same body plan as their larger relatives. Due to their small body size, breathing is easy as oxygen and carbon dioxide have only a very short distance to travel between the surrounding atmosphere and the inside of the insect's body. They also require very little food and moisture to survive. But as they cannot carry or store much energy, quick or energy-intense movement, like flying, is usually done only in short bursts.

Head louse

Head lice are a type of sucking lice that live in human hair. More than a thousand can live on one head, but the normal number is about a dozen. For camouflage they match the colour of the hair in which they live. Anyone can be a host to lice, catching them from other people and clothing. When feeding, the louse grabs a hair and stands on its head, gripping the scalp with a ring of hooks, before inserting a long mouthpart into the skin to suck blood. They feed twice a day, causing irritation and sometimes disease.

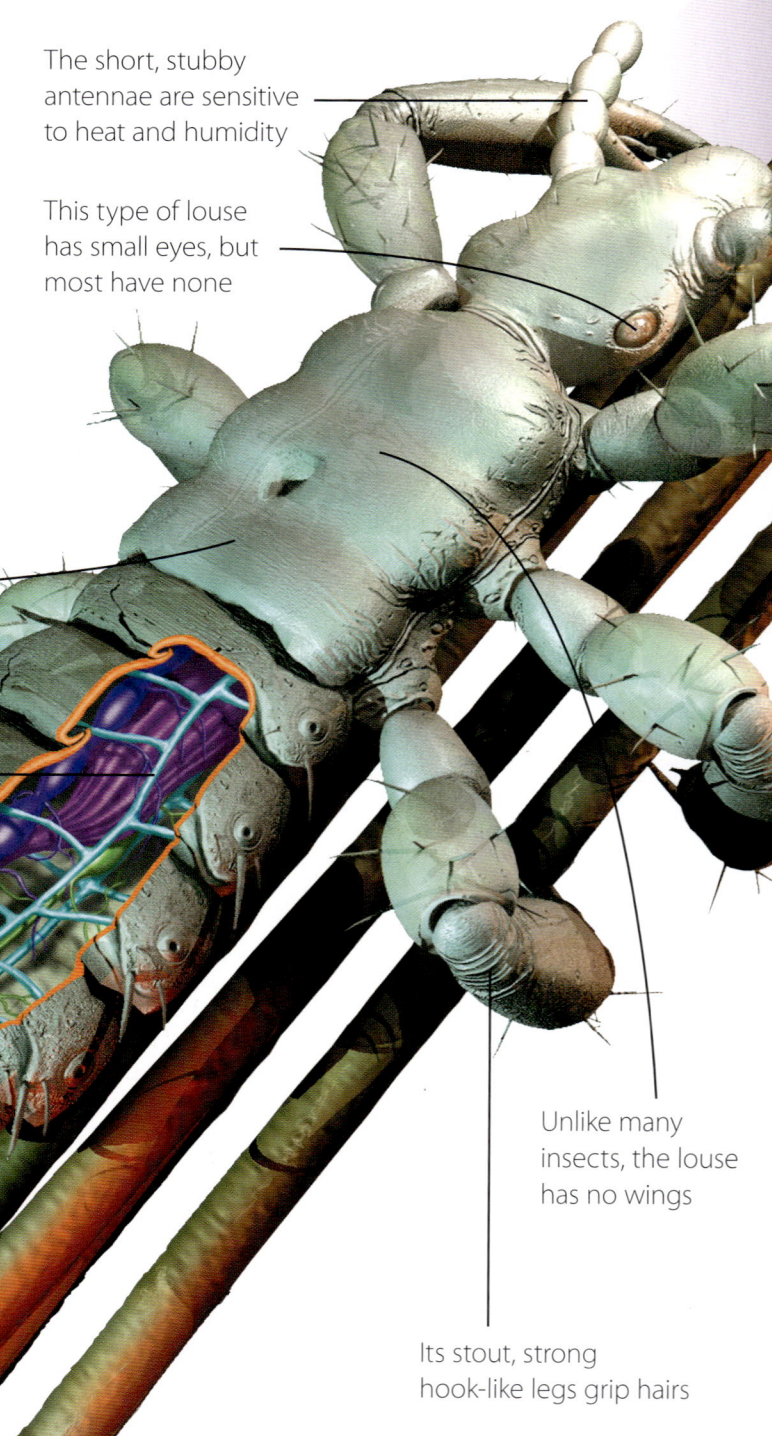

The short, stubby antennae are sensitive to heat and humidity

This type of louse has small eyes, but most have none

Its tough, flattened body makes the louse difficult to remove and very hard to kill

Breathing tubes called trachea take oxygen to and carbon dioxide away from the tissues

The louse's heart pumps blood around its body

The louse appears darker when its intestines are full of digested blood

The nervous system

Spines

Unlike many insects, the louse has no wings

Its stout, strong hook-like legs grip hairs

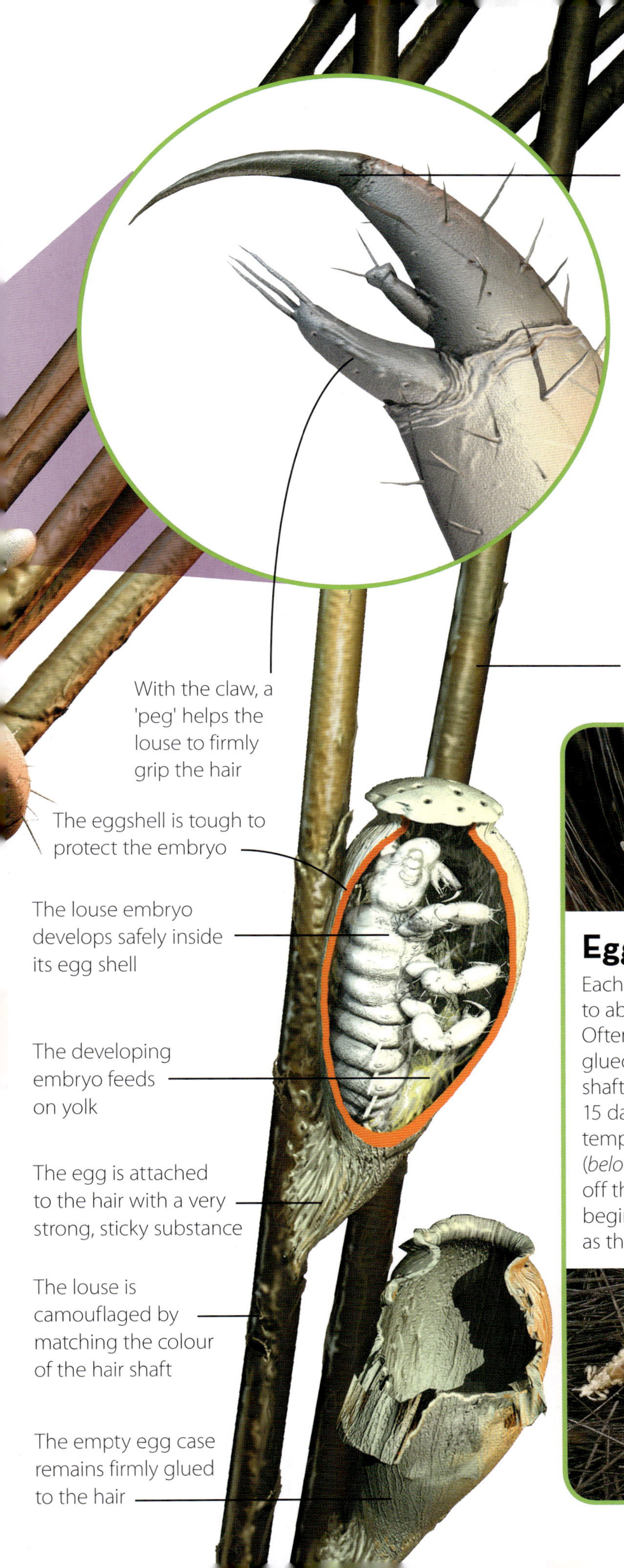

The strong, curved claws can be moved to grip the hair

Climbing feet

A head louse's feet are covered with spines and have curved, hinged claws that grip onto hair with the help of a 'peg'. The claws give the louse a very strong hold and make climbing hair easy. They also make it difficult for the host to remove the louse.

A human hair, viewed through a microscope

With the claw, a 'peg' helps the louse to firmly grip the hair

The eggshell is tough to protect the embryo

The louse embryo develops safely inside its egg shell

The developing embryo feeds on yolk

The egg is attached to the hair with a very strong, sticky substance

The louse is camouflaged by matching the colour of the hair shaft

The empty egg case remains firmly glued to the hair

Eggs

Each day, head lice lay up to about eight eggs (above). Often called 'nits', each is glued very firmly to a hair shaft. The eggs hatch in 6 to 15 days, depending on the temperature. The young lice (below) hatch by pushing off the egg's cap, and they begin to suck blood as soon as they reach the host's skin.

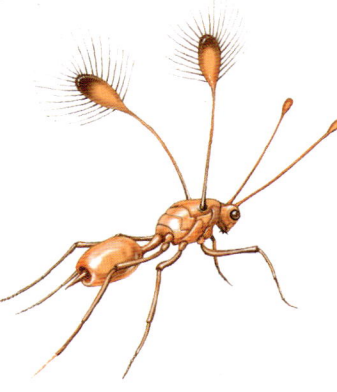

Fairyfly

Less than a quarter of a millimetre long, fairyflies are the smallest of all insects. They are wasps that lay their eggs in other insects. Aquatic species can use their wings for swimming.

Springtail

Springtails can spring several centimetres. Normally the springing organ is tucked under the abdomen, secured by a special hook. When released, it catapults the insect into the air.

Silverfish

Silverfish are covered in fine gleaming scales. They hide away, usually appearing indoors at night to eat paper, leather and food scraps.

Index

A
abdomen 6–9, 15
antennae 6, 8, 12–13, 17, 23, 25, 27, 44
ant lions 42
ant nests 32–33, 36, 37, 42
ants 17, 32–33, 36, 37, 42
anus 22, 23, 24
aphids 32
armour plating 6, 8–9

B
bee nests 34–35
bees 18, 22
beetles 8–12, 14, 17, 20, 18–19, 26–27, 38, 40, 42, 43
blood 6, 22–25, 30, 44
bombardier beetles 18–19
brain 6, 7, 8, 10, 11, 13
breathing 6, 7
bugs 37, 38
bush crickets 22
butterflies 14, 20, 22, 29, 30, 36, 37, 40

C
caecae 23
camouflage 16, 18, 20, 36
caterpillars 18, 21, 28, 30, 31, 32, 42
chemicals 18, 19, 26, 34
chitin 6, 8
chrysalis (pupa) 30–33, 35, 38
cicadas 26
claws 9, 16, 24, 27, 45
cockchafer beetles 12
cockroaches 22–23, 29
colon 22
colour 11, 18, 20–21
crickets 22, 42
crop 6, 23, 25
cuticle 6–9, 13, 14, 18, 20, 30, 42

D
damselflies 11
darkling beetles 42, 43
desert insects 42–43
digestion 6, 7, 22–23, 24
dragonflies 12, 14, 39
dune crickets 42
dung beetles 43

E
eardrums 7
earwigs 12
eggs 12, 24, 26–30, 32–35, 42, 43, 45
epidermis 9
excretion 7, 19
exoskeleton 6, 8, 9, 24
eyes 6, 8, 10–11, 16, 17, 18, 44

F
fairyflies 45
feelers *see antennae*
feet 9, 13, 42
fertilisation 27, 28, 29, 34
fleas 24–25
flies 10, 11, 14
flowers 11, 17
flying 14–15
food 6, 7, 22–23, 24, 32–35

G
galls 40, 41
gizzard 6, 22, 23
glow-worms 26
grasshoppers 7, 36, 43
great diving beetles 38
gut 22, 23, 24, 25

H
hatching 30
head 6, 8, 16, 17
head lice 44–45
heart 6, 44
hinges 9
honey 33, 34, 35
honey bees 34–35
houseflies 22
hunting 16–17

I
ileum 22
intestines 7, 19, 44

J
jaws (mandibles) 6, 8, 16, 17, 18, 25, 39, 42
jewel wasps 43
joints 9, 14

L
lacewings 29, 40
ladybirds 41

larvae 32, 33, 34, 37, 38–39, 40, 41, 43
leaf insects 37
legs 6–9, 15–18, 21, 24, 44
locusts 6–7, 43

M
mandibles *see jaws*
mantises 16–17, 36
mating 26–27, 32
maxilla 8
mayflies 38
microscopic life 44–45
mosquitoes 22, 38
moths 12, 18, 26, 40, 41
moulting 30, 31
mouth 6, 8, 11, 22
muscles 8, 9, 14, 17, 19, 25

N
nectar 34
nerve cells 7, 10
nymphs 38, 39

O
ocelli 10
oesophagus 22, 25
ommatidia 10, 11
oocytes 28, 29
optic nerves 11
ovaries 26, 27, 28

P
parasites 24–25
poison 18, 36, 37
pollen 34, 35
pond skaters 39
praying mantises 16–17
pupa *see chrysalis*

R
rainforests 38–39
rectum 7, 19, 22, 24, 25
rhabdom 10

S
saliva 22, 23, 25
sawflies 12, 29, 41
scales 21
segments 8
self-defence 18–19
sense organs 8, 12
sensory cells 13

sensory pegs 13
shield bugs 37
silverfish 45
sperm 24, 26, 27, 28
spines 18, 36
spotted flower beetle 8
springtails 12, 39, 45
stag beetles 17
stick insects 21, 29
sting 18, 42

T
tarsus 9
taste hairs 23
termites 12, 18, 37
testes 26, 27
thorax 8, 14, 15, 17, 22
thornbugs 36
tiger beetles 17, 42
trachea 6, 44
tree hoppers 36

U
uterus 26, 27

V
vagina 24

W
waggle dance 35
wasps 12, 14–15, 42, 43, 45
waste 22, 23
water boatmen 39
water insects 38–39
water scorpions 29
weevils 12, 40
whirligig beetles 10, 11, 38
wings 7, 8, 9, 14–15, 16, 20, 21, 30
woodland life 40–41

Z
zygotes 29